365 Ways To Get You Writing

Other titles for creative writers from How To Books.

LIKELY STORIES

Fabulous, inspirational, chuckleworthy and deeeply instructive tales about creative writing as told to the author by his ubiquitous Guru

Hugh Scott

Whitbread winning author

HOW TO WRITE A CHILDREN'S PICTURE BOOK AND GET IT PUBLISHED

Andrea Shavick

HOW TO WRITE FOR TELEVISION

A guide to writing and selling successful TV scripts

William Smethurst

HOW TO WRITE GREAT SCREENPLAYS

And get them into production

William Smethurst

HOW TO WRITE YOUR FIRST NOVEL

Sophie King

THE FIVE-MINUTE WRITER

Exercise and inspiration in creative writing in five minutes a day

Margret Geraghty

Write or phone for a catalogue to:

How To Books
Spring Hill House
Spring Hill Road
Begbroke
Oxford
OX5 1RX
Tel. 01865 375794

Or email: info@howtobooks.co.uk

Visit our website www.howtobooks.co.uk
to find out more about us and our books.

Like our Facebook page How To Books & Spring Hill

Follow us on Twitter @Howtobooksltd

Read our books online www.howto.co.uk

365 Ways To Get **You** WRITING

DAILY INSPIRATION and ADVICE for Creative WRITERS

Jane COOPER

howtobooks

Published by How To Books Ltd
Spring Hill House, Spring Hill Road
Begbroke, Oxford OX5 1RX United Kingdom
Tel: (01865) 375794
Fax: (01865) 379162
info@howtobooks.co.uk
www.howtobooks.co.uk

The right of Jane Cooper to be identified as author of this work has been
asserted by her in accordance with the Copyright, Designs and Patents Act
1988.

British Library Cataloguing in Publication Data
A catalogue record for this book is available from the British Library

ISBN: 978 1 84528 492 3

Produced for How To Books by Deer Park Productions, Tavistock, Devon
Typeset by PDQ Typesetting Ltd, Newcastle-under-Lyme, Staffordshire
Printed and bound in Great Britain by Bell & Bain Ltd, Glasgow

NOTE: The material contained in this book is set out in good faith for general
guidance and no liability can be accepted for loss or expense incurred as a
result of relying in particular circumstances on statements made in the book.
Laws and regulations are complex and liable to change, and readers should
check the current position with the relevant authorities before making personal
arrangements.

CONTENTS

Contents

CONTENTS

Contents

Contents

CONTENTS

INTRODUCTION

A publisher once told me that while the most common New Year's resolution is to lose weight, the second most common is to take up writing. So, if so many people intend to do it, why aren't we all writing all the time?

There are two reasons: sometimes you don't know what to write, and sometimes you don't know how to write well. (On a really bad day you might have both problems at once. If so, walk to a coffee shop to read a book and eat a comforting slice of cake.)

This book aims to help you with both these tribulations. Each two-page spread lets you tackle a new topic. Some of these will give you ideas, so you don't sit facing a blank page. Some will guide you through specific aspects of writing skill.

Many creative writing books will give you a whole chapter of explanation and examples, and then just one little task to try at the end. Many other creative writing books are just strings of exercises.

This book is different. While most of the mini-chapters have four tasks for you try (and some have even more) they also all begin with a little bit of advice, an example, or some support. Each page spread also ends with suggestions of how you could take your work further.

Our first skill is a key one that I promise you will improve everything else you write. Turn the page to start your journey from New Year's resolution to next New Year's Eve.

SHOW, DON'T TELL 1

Grasping a basic skill that will improve everything else you write

'Show, don't tell', is a phrase you will often hear writing tutors use. It means that you have to leave a little work for your readers to do. Instead of telling them, '*She felt tense,*' show her nails digging into the palms of her hands. Rather than explicitly saying, '*He found the letter confusing,*' show your readers that he is reading and re-reading it.

Beware of adverbs; they tell your reader too much. Don't tell your reader that a child, '*spoke cheekily,*' give the child cheeky words to say. Don't emphasise that the tenor, '*sang powerfully,*' show us that a woman in the audience is wiping a tear from her eye as the aria finishes, or that the glass drops in the chandelier are vibrating.

For these exercises you'll need to keep coming back to these three basic sentences:

I came into the room. I saw Alan. I greeted him and sat down.

You must always keep the same basic ideas – an entry, an encounter, and a greeting. Stick to first person and past tense too. But, by changing the verbs, show these different emotions and relationships.

SHOW, DON'T TELL 1

1   *Rewrite the three sentences to show that the speaker is angry with Alan.*

2   *Rewrite the three sentences to show that the speaker is afraid of Alan.*

3   *Rewrite the three sentences to show that the speaker finds Alan very attractive.*

4   *Rewrite the three sentences to show that the speaker is surprised to find Alan there.*

What would happen to your groups of sentences if they were about a woman called Alice rather than a man called Alan? How would that change the ways you show these emotions?

You, The Writer

Taking time to consider how you began writing, and on what keeps you going

When I first began to write, my only ally was Petra, my teddy bear. We shared a bedroom with my two younger sisters and we needed a bolthole until I was old enough to start primary school.

My dad's armchair sat across the corner of the sitting room at an angle, leaving a wedge of space behind. I'd reverse in there each morning, pulling behind me an old, round, red, tin tray. On the tray sat Petra, my pencils, and my writing pad – a bundle of torn-off envelope backs my mum had punched holes in and tied together with string. I covered the pages with what I called stories, but were really just sagging lines of malformed letter Xs, over and over again.

I was writing before I could write, writing before I could read, writing for an audience of one, a hug-flattened bear who'd already had both his shiny eyes loved off. That's where it all began for me.

5 *What is your first memory that involves writing? Is it about learning to write at all, as a skill, or is it about learning to make up stories?*

6 *What memories do you have of how others have reacted to your writing? Can you recall specific praise, or criticism? How have you responded to this?*

7 *Which piece of writing have you been most satisfied with once it was finished? Why? Has anyone else read it? What was their response?*

8 *Which piece of writing have you found hardest to complete, or been least satisfied with once it was finished? Why? Are there pieces that you could not finish at all? Why?*

If you'd like to find out how one ordinary kid became a best-selling author, and pick up some writing advice along the way, read *On Writing* by Stephen King.

Lovely Lists 1

Using lists to make you see things differently

I love lists. Nothing makes me happier than a nice 'to do' list with lots of items cheerfully crossed off in a different colour. I've even been known to add simple little tasks to my list, just so I can cross them out quickly and look purposeful.

These lists are different. Spend a few minutes on each one. Let your imagination, and your love of language, lead you. Try to write something nobody else would think of. Be delightfully oblique. What gets kissed? It better. What was I given by age ten? A good few tellings off. What doesn't have corners? Scrambled egg!

9	*Make a list of things you have lost.*

10	*Make a list of things that do not have corners.*

LOVELY LISTS 1

11 *Make a list of things you were given by the age of ten.*

12 *Make a list of things that get kissed.*

What would you like to do with these lists now? Make them into a poem? Give some of the ideas and experiences in them to a character you're writing about? Turn one item on the list into the start of a story plot?

You'll find more chances to make curious lists later in the book.

Meanwhile, you might like to read a list made by a fictional character. In the final chapter of *The Great Gatsby*, after Gatsby has died, his father finds a list his son made as a teenager. Gatsby's good intentions, including that he will, '*Read one improving book or magazine per week,*' and '*Be better to parents,*' are terribly poignant in the light of his later life and sudden, violent death.

THE RULES

Exploring whether there are rules for writing, and how they can help you

I sometimes get school pupils to write poetry. I show them examples. I offer them inspirations. I give them time to gather ideas. Then, just before they write, I ask them if they have any questions, and someone always asks me: *'Does it have to rhyme?'*

We love the idea that there might be rules that will make our work turn out just right. And, there's no shortage of advice out there.

---

13 *Elmore Leonard, author of* Get Shorty *and* Be Cool *famously listed his ten rules of writing. You can find these easily on the internet. Which rule do you agree with most? Are there any you strongly disagree with? Why?*

---

14 *Head back to the internet again and look for Allan Guthrie's list of writing rules called* 'Hunting Down The Pleonasms'. *Which rule do you agree with most? Are there any you strongly disagree with? Why?*

---

15 *Broadcaster Sue MacGregor, when judging the BBC National Short Story Competition, said stories need, 'great intensity...there's no time to build up to anything.' Fellow judge Joe Dunthorne added, 'You're always looking for no wasted sentences and no wasted words...There's no way you can get away with a clunky paragraph in a short story.' Do you agree? Why?*

16 *What would you tell my pupils about rhyme? What do you think the rules of poetry are?*

You can always learn from these rules – they became the rules for a reason. If something in your writing is not working, the rules might help you work out why. But in the end, what works is what works, whether it fits somebody's rule or not.

SEEING THE OBJECT

Finding new ways to examine and describe familiar things

In his poem *'A Martian Sends A Postcard Home'*, Craig Raine shows us the world from an alien's point of view. Many familiar objects become almost unrecognisable. The visitor's lack of Earth experience means he calls the telephone a *'haunted apparatus'*, perhaps because of the disembodied voices he hears coming from it. To him, a book is a bird because it perches on the hand, and a bathroom is a torture cell of strange sounds and noises.

These tasks will get you to bring out the rich strangeness in everyday objects by seeing them through different eyes.

17 *Go to the kitchen and find a useful piece of equipment. Describe it as if you are a scientist analysing it for the first time.*

18 *Pick up an ornament or holiday souvenir. Describe it as if you are an alien who has just arrived on Earth.*

19 *Go to your garage or the cupboard where you keep tools and paint pots. Find an item designed for a useful purpose. Describe it as if you are a young child.*

20 *Finally, choose an object with which you are very familiar, something that has been extremely useful, or has great sentimental value. Now describe it as if you are actually quite afraid of or disturbed by it.*

If you'd like one more challenge, try rewriting one of these descriptions to use just half as many adjectives.

SENSES 1

Bringing all five senses into your writing

You'll find a number of reminders in this book about bringing all the senses into your writing. D W Wilson, who won the BBC National Short Story Competition with his tale *The Dead Roads*, said in an interview, *'I just try and hit all five of the senses once every two pages. It's a rule that's just ingrained. I just do it . . . to try and make it visceral, to try and make it authentic.'*

Because this is such an important skill, we're going to focus on it in isolation now. If you Google *'sherbet lemon game'* you'll find an exercise schoolteachers love to use to get pupils writing sensually. You can play this writing game with any food that has an interesting 'wrapping' round it – a boiled sweet in a crackling wrapper, a crinkly packet of crisps, a peach in its velvet skin or an artisan loaf sold in a brown paper bag. You'll need to have the wrapped food in front of you before you begin. Don't touch it yet.

21 *Describe what you can see as vividly as possible.*

22 *Now pick it up in one hand, keeping your pen in the other. Write about what you feel. Think about its hardness or softness, and its texture.*

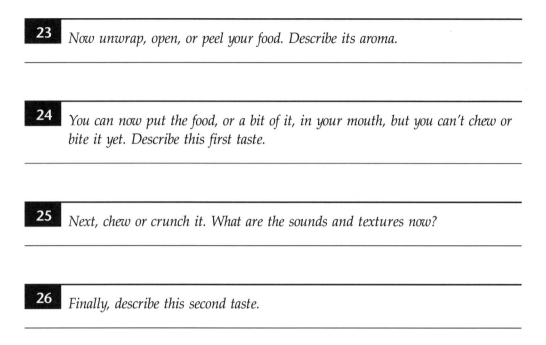

23 *Now unwrap, open, or peel your food. Describe its aroma.*

24 *You can now put the food, or a bit of it, in your mouth, but you can't chew or bite it yet. Describe this first taste.*

25 *Next, chew or crunch it. What are the sounds and textures now?*

26 *Finally, describe this second taste.*

You'll get another opportunity to focus on the senses later. Lots of the other tasks in this book will also remind you to bring all the senses into what you write.

A Short Story

Producing complete short fiction in four simple steps

As we've seen already, lots of people will try to tell you there are rules about how to write a short story. You might even believe them. Then you'll read a story that you love, and that you think works, but it'll break some of the rules. In the end, the only rule really is: if it works, it works.

However, here's one rule: in a successful short story, something should have changed by the end. You're going to follow this rule by writing a complete short story in just FOUR paragraphs. And, each paragraph can be only THREE sentences long.

27   *Write a first paragraph in which the main character is going somewhere.*

28   *Write a second paragraph in which the main character overhears something that grabs their interest or seems important.*

A Short Story

---

29 *Write a third paragraph in which the main character reacts to, thinks about, or reflects upon what he/she has heard.*

---

30 *Write a fourth paragraph in which the main character has a change of direction or plan.*

Even in this very basic version of a short story, change can mean different things. It can be an actual change of travel direction. It can be something more internal – a change of heart, a change of plan, a change in something your main character believes.

Does your tiny and basic story have the potential to be fleshed out into something more developed?

DESCRIPTIONS 1

Describing vividly, without overdoing it

Description is one of the building block skills of writing. If you want your reader to get lost in the world you create, you need to make that world, and everything in it, seem real.

Do be careful with adjectives and adverbs. The bright teenagers I work with often write things like this: '*The slow, green river slipped lazily and quietly through the silent, verdant forest. Tiny, mischievous monkeys scampered cheekily from one lofty, majestic tree to the next.*' Putting too many adjectives and adverbs in your writing is like putting too much butter icing on your cupcakes: people soon start to feel just a little nauseous.

It's easy to write a visual description, to say what something looks like. Try to get other senses into your descriptions too.

31 *Describe the monster that lives under the bed or in the wardrobe.*

32 *Describe a firework display.*

Descriptions 1

---

33 *Choose a piece of clothing you are very fond of. Describe it without using any adjectives. (Similes and metaphors might help you here.)*

---

34 *Describe the sky outside your window right now. Come back at a different time of day and describe it again.*

All of these tasks have made you write what we might call objective descriptions, which tell us what something is just plainly like. Later in this book you'll have an opportunity to try writing much more subjective, even biased, descriptions.

The First Time 1

Recalling significant personal experiences to inform your writing

Ewan MacColl's song *The First Time Ever I Saw Your Face* has been covered by Roberta Flack, Johnny Cash and X Factor winner Leona Lewis. Pulp asked *Do You Remember The First Time?*

First times are massively memorable. Psychologists have identified the 'primacy effect', our tendency to remember first things on a list rather than later items. You probably can't remember what you did at work every day for the last month, but I'm sure you remember your first day in that job, with all the hopes and anxieties it brought.

These tasks will all get you to remember first times. What did you think, or feel? What do remember seeing, smelling, tasting, touching, or hearing? Was the experience what you had expected it would be?

35   *Write about the first time you flew in a plane.*

36   *Write about the first time you stole something.*

37 *Write about the first time you kissed someone.*

38 *If you've done it, write about the first time you smoked or took drugs.*

What could you do with these firsts? You might give one of them to a character in a story. If so, you've got the freedom to let them experience the event a little differently. Your character could be brave where you were afraid, or foolish where you were wise.

You've been thinking about first times, but is there anything you think you may have done for the **last** time? How do you feel about that?

PICTURE PEOPLE 1
Using photographs to help you create characters

There's a fantastic character sketch in William McIlvanney's short story *Death of a Spinster*. The way the woman is described absolutely shows her rigid, controlled nature.

> *Each weekday was mapped. When the digital alarm went, she would press the snooze mechanism two separate times so that she would have about ten minutes more in bed. When she got out of bed, she would reset the alarm for next day, making sure each time it was set for a.m. Tomorrow was promised.*
>
> *The day took her to itself like an assembly line ... She showered, wearing the floral shower-cap ... She dried and dressed in the clothes she had laid out the previous evening.*
>
> *She clicked on the already-filled kettle. She turned on the gas till it clicked alight and put on it the two eggs waiting in their panful of water. She gave the eggs three minutes from the time the water boiled. She toasted one slice of bread and buttered it. She poured the hot water into the cup containing instant coffee and one sweetener. She put one egg, taken out of the pan with a tablespoon and dried with a teacloth, into an eggcup and the other in the saucer beside it. She breakfasted.*

For these exercises you should start by finding some photos in newspapers or magazines of people you think look interesting. Don't pick anyone you recognise – you don't want any preconceived ideas in your head.

Picture People 1

You're going to write in third person (using *he/she*), and in detail, to describe your character doing a simple task. The way you describe the character and his or her actions should reveal as much as possible about what this person is like. Use as little dialogue as possible – none if you can.

39 *Write a piece in which your character goes shopping for an outfit to wear to a wedding.*

40 *Describe your character ordering and eating a meal alone in a restaurant.*

42 *Describe this person waiting for a badly delayed bus.*

This is a technique you can use again and again in your writing. Actions always speak louder than words.

If you want to read the rest of the story, a tiny and heart-breaking gem, you'll find it in William McIlvanney's collection *Walking Wounded*.

UNEXPECTED

Beginning stories with unexpected events

If you grew up in the 1980s like I did, you'll remember the strangely hypnotic music, and the curvaceous woman dancing in the flames. Roald Dahl's *Tales Of The Unexpected* puzzled and intrigued me, and I went on to read most of the stories the TV programme was based on.

His stories often ended with the startling, with a twist or shock. These tasks, however, will get you to start with the unexpected. Use these beginnings to challenge your characters and get their stories moving.

---

43 *I don't like art galleries, and I was very bored in this one, trying to eat a bar of chocolate without any of the guards seeing me. Suddenly, out of the corner of my eye, I noticed something move in one of the paintings. I looked closer.*

---

44 *I went to get Ben for his morning walk. Instead of our dog, the basket held a tiny, spiky-tailed dinosaur.*

---

45   *I was browsing the shelves when a book tumbled off into my hands, already open at a certain page. The heading at the top read, 'How To Get Revenge Without Anyone Knowing'.*

---

46   *I was rather surprised to wake up that morning and find I had somehow become a human-sized spider overnight. How was I to get downstairs without scaring my mother half to death?*

How did your characters cope with these challenges?

If you'd like to read some of Dahl's tales, two of the most justifiably famous are *The Landlady* and *Lamb to the Slaughter*. My favourite one, though, is *The Way Up To Heaven*, which contains a crime so perfect no one would ever know it had been committed, and a victim so deserving you'll rub your hands with glee when he meets his fate.

CHILDHOOD

Drawing on childhood memories to use in your writing

Graham Greene said that childhood was *'the writer's bank balance'*. Flannery O'Connor wrote, *'Anybody who has survived his childhood has enough information about life to last him the rest of his days.'* Our childhoods are full of stories, events and observations that we can use in our writing.

47 *Write about a party you remember from childhood. Who was there? What games did you play? What did you eat? What presents were given? What did you wear?*

48 *What advice were you given as a child? Did you ever follow any of it? What do you think of that advice now?*

49 *Can you remember learning to ride a bike? Who taught you? How did you master that skill?*

50 *Write about a childhood incident that filled you with dread.*

What you have written so far is probably an absolutely true account, as well as you can remember it. Don't be afraid to polish what you've written. You can adapt it, make it more fictional, or put it in the life of a character you've created.

Novelists have always understood the power of stories about childhood and coming of age. Trezza Azzopardi's *The Hiding Place* tells the story of Dol, the youngest of an impoverished, Maltese, immigrant family in Cardiff in the early 1960s. Fostered away from the family at an early age, she is only now reconstructing her childhood memories and coming to understand some terrible family secrets. In Michael Frayn's *Spies*, elderly Englishman Stephen Wheatley recalls spying on a friend's mother one wartime summer.

START IN THE MIDDLE

Getting straight to the point, and moving on from there

The young writers I work with often want to put far too much unnecessary detail at the start of their stories. They tell me about their character waking up, getting dressed, eating breakfast, having a phone call, and getting ready to go out. Only then do they let me find out about the amazing things that happen to the character once he or she is out in the world.

These prompts will get you to start at a dramatic point and take the story on from there. There are other chances in this book to work on flashbacks, but this time I really want you to resist using this technique. Start where the prompt puts you, and keep going forward from there.

51 *Start a story with a character already trapped in a cupboard or wardrobe. Don't flash back to how they got there, just keep going forwards.*

52 *Start a story with a character already hanging from the edge of a roof by his or her fingertips. Don't flash back to how they got there, just take the story forwards.*

---

53   *Start a story with a character already precariously balanced on a plank. Don't flash back to how they got there, just take the story forwards.*

---

54   *Start a story with a character already hiding behind the counter of a bank, post office, or shop. Don't flash back to how they got there, just take the story forwards.*

Did you resist the urge of the flashback? How long did it take you to get your character out of the opening predicament? And what did you do to him or her next? Was that the end of the story, or did you fling a new and bigger challenge in the character's path?

If your stories did just solve the opening problem, go back to at least one of them to create a longer tale in which the challenges get bigger and tougher.

SIMILES

Creating your own striking similes

I love similes, those comparisons when one thing is brought to life by its being *like* or *as* another thing. I was trying to persuade my husband that raspberries are hairy. He was unconvinced, but we were sitting in the cinema waiting for the film to start and couldn't just go and look at the ones we'd bought at the farmers' market that morning. Then it came to me. Raspberries are hairy, I told him, like a granny's chin.

Craig Easton and Brigid Benson's enticing travel book *52 Weekends by the Sea* has some lovely similes. The writers describe, *'newly-sheared sheep like roughly peeled potatoes'* and rockfall from the cliffs as being, *'like smashed digestive biscuits'*.

These tasks will get you creating your own similes.

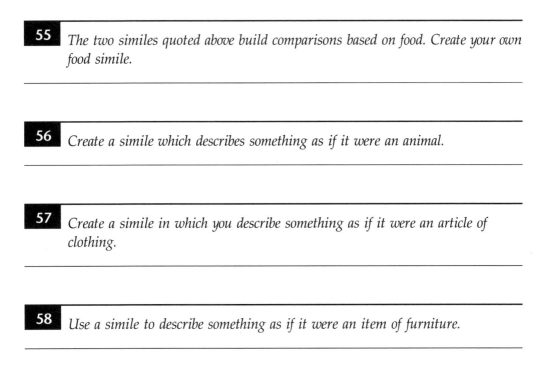

55 *The two similes quoted above build comparisons based on food. Create your own food simile.*

56 *Create a simile which describes something as if it were an animal.*

57 *Create a simile in which you describe something as if it were an article of clothing.*

58 *Use a simile to describe something as if it were an item of furniture.*

If you've enjoyed working with similes, I recommend a book called *Eyes Like Butterflies*. It's a collection of similes and metaphors collected by Terence Hodgson. He began gathering them when he was struck by a character in a novel who was said to have *'a voice like hundreds and thousands'*. He noted this image down, and spent years assembling thousands of others, which he arranged by theme. If you'd like to see how nineteen writers described noses, or read eight pages of ways to explore a smile, they're all in there.

GOOGLEWHACK

Playing an internet word game to stretch your vocabulary

A googlewhack is what happens when two words are entered into Google, without any quotation marks round them, and it comes back with one and only one hit. The comedian Dave Gorman was once told that his website contained a googlewhack, *Francophile namesakes*. This eventually led to a round the world journey, a stand-up show, and a best-selling book as he went off in pursuit of other googlewhacks.

There are a number of internet sites listing googlewhacks (which, if you think about it, must sort of invalidate them by repeating them on a second site). Listed there you'll find such odd expressions as *hittable preteenager*, and *weirdly psychobiographic* as well as my favourite: *netherworldly comediennes*.

In these tasks you are going to try to create googlewhacks and use them to inspire your writing. If you want to, you can be terribly scrupulous and check the internet to see if you do really just get one hit. It's all right though if you just build unlikely phrases and then let yourself be provoked by them. They can become titles, subjects, or themes for what you go on to write.

59 *Create a googlewhack from an animal and part of a car. Write a piece inspired by your combination.*

60 *Create a googlewhack from any object you can see from where you are writing, and a critical adjective. Write a piece inspired by your combination.*

61 *Create a googlewhack from something you owned when you were a child, and a scientific or technical word. Write a piece inspired by your combination.*

62 *Create a googlewhack from a foreign food and a plant, flower, or tree. Write a piece inspired by your combination.*

Even if your phrases didn't turn out to be true and unique googlewhacks, they should, I hope, have got you having fun with the stretchy possibilities of language.

A Bad Beginning

Writing bad beginnings to learn how to write good ones

The Victorian novelist Edward Bulwer-Lytton wrote one of the most famous opening lines in literature, '*It was a dark and stormy night.*' Sadly, he spoiled it by not stopping there. Lytton's opening sentence went on for another 51 tortured words. '*It was a dark and stormy night; the rain fell in torrents – except at occasional intervals, when it was checked by a violent gust of wind which swept up the streets (for it is in London that our scene lies), rattling along the housetops, and fiercely agitating the scanty flame of the lamps that struggled against the darkness.*'

In his honour, the annual Bulwer-Lytton first line competition invites participants to make up and send in terrible opening sentences for novels. The 2011 winner, Sue Fondrie, wrote this: '*Cheryl's mind turned like the vanes of a wind-powered turbine, chopping her sparrow-like thoughts into bloody pieces that fell onto a growing pile of forgotten memories.*'

These tasks will get you to write your own bad beginnings. Each sentence you write must be the possible first line of a novel or short story. Each must be grammatically correct and linguistically perfect. Each one should be deliberately and gloriously terrible.

63 *Write a purposely atrocious opening sentence for a thriller or action adventure novel.*

64 *Create a terrible start for a detective novel.*

65 *Write the thoroughly awful beginning of a romance.*

66 *Let rip with a ghastly start for a work of historical fiction.*

67 *Come up with a bad start to a science fiction story.*

Why have we been indulging in this nonsense? Because if you can recognise what's bad, you won't write rubbish by accident when you're trying to be good.

CHANGING TENSE

Rewriting in a different tense to see what's most effective

Hilary Mantel's Booker Prize winning novel, *Wolf Hall*, tells the story of Thomas Cromwell, Henry VIII's right-hand man, in present tense. Over 650 pages she unfolds 35 years of history before our eyes. Her choice of tense makes us feel we are watching characters rise and fall in the Tudor court.

Present tense can also be a useful tense for detective stories and thrillers. It lets the reader experience the action, and the revelations, at the same time as the characters, increasing the sense of drama or surprise.

Present tense narrative does have limitations. It's inflexible, and makes it far harder to move in and out of flashbacks. It can make every sentence sound like a stage direction: *Janice walks up to the bar and orders a mojito.* It can make your readers feel claustrophobic, as if they can't step back from the characters and events.

English has many more tenses that you can play with. (And, in fact, more tenses than many other languages.) It gives you the power to say what happened once, what usually happened, what was happening at the time, what had happened before something else happened, what might happen later, what actually did happen later, what may well happen, and so on. Do you want to cut yourself off from all these possibilities?

CHANGING TENSE

68 *Find a piece of fiction that has been written in past tense. Rewrite the first few paragraphs in present tense. How is this better? What have you gained or improved? How is this worse? What have you lost?*

69 *Find a piece of fiction that has been written in present tense. Rewrite the first few paragraphs in past tense. How is this better? What have you gained or improved? How is this worse? What have you lost?*

If you're trying to write something that isn't working, one way to shake it up might be to change your tense from past to present, or vice versa.

If you want to explore more novels written in present tense, try *The Time Traveler's Wife* by Audrey Niffenegger or *Rabbit, Run* by John Updike.

NEUROSES

Exploring fears and habits to determine your characters' actions

Psychologists would say that a neurosis is a socially acceptable behaviour that is taken just a step too far. It's perfectly logical to be careful while walking down stairs, but it's rather neurotic of me to clutch the rail in case I miss a step and tumble to the ground in a broken heap. There's nothing wrong with making sure you've turned the gas off, but it's neurotic to go back and check it again and again.

We all have our little neuroses and they cause us distress. They are our 'invisible injuries'. These prompts will get you to consider yours.

70 *Write about your greatest fear. This might be a fear of something genuinely catastrophic, or it might be a small and illogical fear that nonetheless looms large for you.*

71 *What neurotic little habits do you have? What do they reveal about you?*

---

72 *What stops you being able to relax?*

---

73 *What stops you sleeping, or wakes you in the night?*

Now that you've thought about these neuroses, what are you going to use them for?

At the end of George Orwell's *1984*, his hero Winston Smith is tortured in Room 101 with the threat of what he fears most – rats. His neurosis is used to break him.

You could give your fear, habit or impediment to a character in a story. How does it affect their life? You could put your character in a situation where the only way to deal with the challenges ahead of them is to confront their neurosis. You might face your character with their greatest fear and watch what happens. For a writer, all of life is potential material.

PARENT AND CHILD 1

Taking inspiration from a fundamental relationship

Our relationship with our parents is our first, and one of our most significant. For those who later become parents, nothing seems to be so deep, so complex, or so unbreakable as the bond with their children. Conversations between parents and children can be the most touching in the world, but also the angriest, or the most complex.

Decide whether you want to tackle these as scripts, or as narratives. You might feel each one deserves a slightly different approach.

---

74 *Write about a parent trying to explain the facts of life to a child. Who starts the conversation? Is anyone embarrassed? Are they blunt, or do they speak very delicately?*

---

75 *A teenager wants to be allowed to go off on holiday with a gang of friends. How does he/she try to persuade a parent? How does the parent try to resist, or what conditions does the parent lay down?*

---

76   *A child has done something very naughty while his or her parents were out. What did he/she do? Is the child confessing and apologising, or making excuses, or perhaps even lying and trying to cover it all up?*

---

77   *Write about a parental argument from a child's point of view. What did the child hear or see? How much has the child actually understood of what was going on between the parents?*

Read back over your work. What would happen if you changed the mood of one of these? What would happen if you made the parent respond differently to what the child says?

As the parent–child relationship is such a rich one, we'll come back to it again later in the book.

ADJECTIVES AND NOUNS

Making startling combinations to shake loose your imagination

Juxtapositions – surprising combinations of words you wouldn't normally put together – can be inspiring.

To get ready for these writing tasks, prepare some words, preferably a few days before you need them. This will make the words, and the combinations, more startling when you use them.

You need a varied group of adjectives (describing words) and a varied group of nouns (naming words). Write each word on a different card. You could even use one colour for adjectives and one for nouns. Shuffle your two piles of cards and place them face down. Come back to them in a few days.

78 *Pick one adjective and one noun, e.g.* angry + teapot; quivering + possum. *Now imagine this is the title of a blockbuster Hollywood movie. Write the voiceover for the trailer.*

79 *Pick one adjective and one noun, e.g.* magic + end; doubtful + lamp. *Now imagine this is the title of a murder mystery novel. Write the blurb for the back of the book jacket.*

---

80   *Pick one adjective and one noun, e.g.* tiny + box; surprising + clock. *Now imagine this is the title of a book for very young children. Write the first few pages of the story.*

---

81   *Pick one adjective and one noun, e.g.* fluffy + spiral; shameful + diamond. *Now imagine this is the title of a romantic novel. Write the last page of the book, in which the hero and heroine finally declare their love for each other.*

This is a great exercise to do with a group of writers, perhaps at the start of a session as a warm-up. If everyone brings their own pile of word cards you can have endless permutations. You can probably come up with more ways to write about the combinations too.

SUBTEXTS

Showing what lies beneath the surface of a conversation

A really well-written conversation will nearly always have a subtext, something going on below the surface, something to do with the mood the characters are in, or with the state of the relationship between them. While the actual words of their conversation will say one thing, the subtext may say quite another. The subtext may reveal tensions, unspoken desires, fears and so on.

STOP! Before you read any further on, pick a number from 1 to 4 and a letter from A to D. Write them down. Do the same thing three more times, until you've used all the letters and numbers. Done that? Good. Now read on...

Speech situations:
1   X and Y start chatting while waiting for the bus.
2   X is a shop assistant in an expensive boutique. Y has come in to buy an outfit to wear to a job interview.
3   Middle-aged X is trying to persuade parent-in-law Y that it is time to move into residential care.
4   X and Y used to work together. They haven't seen each other for a while until they meet at another ex-colleague's retirement party.

Subtexts:
A   X feels very uncomfortable with Y and is afraid of making Y angry.
B   X wants to get the conversation over as quickly as possible without actually seeming rude.
C   X is secretly afraid s/he might be suffering from the same illness that killed his/her mother.
D   Y is preoccupied with work and not really paying much attention to the conversation.

82 *Now write a scene of conversation between X and Y, using the first of your number/letter combinations. This can be pure dialogue as a section of playscript or screenplay, or can be part of a piece of prose fiction with narration and description around it.*

83 *Now write a scene of conversation between X and Y using the second of your combinations.*

84 *Use the third of your combinations to write another scene of conversation between X and Y.*

85 *And now do one more scene of conversation using the last of your combinations.*

You've only been asked to write single scenes so far. How might these fit into the wider script of a whole play? What could have happened in the earlier scenes? What might happen in the later ones?

FLASHBACKS 1

Working out what brought your characters to a certain point

I love books about polar exploration. Recently I read *Call of the White* by Felicity Aston, in which she explains how she led an eight-woman team to the South Pole. The book begins with a catastrophic storm that destroyed one of their two tents, leaving them in grave danger. Then she flashes back to the start of the story, telling us how the idea for the expedition came to her, and how her team was recruited and trained.

You're going to see four dramatic openings. Write the flashback that tells your reader how the character ended up in this tricky position.

86 *Just as my granny had always warned me, the wind had changed and my face had stuck like that. Now how was I going to get through the day with my nose twisted up and my tongue sticking out?*

87 *'If he comes any closer,' I thought. 'I'll scream.' He came closer.*

88 *When I woke, the jungle was quiet except for the sound of dangerous snoring. What I had mistaken in the dark for a mound of grass and leaves was actually the biggest lion I had ever seen in my life.*

89 *A key turned in the lock. My cell door opened. A scene of total devastation met my eyes. I heard the door clanging shut and the evil cackling of the guard. I was alone in this barren place.*

In Aston's book we have to wait a long time before we find out how they deal with the loss of that vital tent. When we get to that point again, the story carries on from there to its eventual ending. You've been asked to write the flashback that comes before the gripping opening. Which story or stories could you complete right through to the end?

SHOWING THOUGHT

Letting readers see what characters are thinking

The young writers I work with sometimes have trouble letting their readers know what a character is thinking. Their problem is that they make it seem as if our thoughts come out in perfectly made sentences. They write things like. *'Oh dear,' he thought. 'I'll never get to work on time. My boss is going to be furious.'*

We don't think this way, however, and it feels unnatural to read it. It would be better if they wrote the scenario like this: *He'd never get to work in time. His boss would be furious.* This puts the reader in the position of following the character's thoughts, and does not force us to believe that anyone thinks in neatly organised full sentences.

As you try these tasks, keep remembering to show as much as possible and not to overtell.

---

90   *Use the following phrase to start a piece of writing: Looking round the dinner table he/she...*

---

91   *Use the following phrase to start a piece of writing: Gazing at the trees outside he/she...*

SHOWING THOUGHT

---

92 *Use the following phrase to start a piece of writing: Pushing his way along the corridor he/she...*

---

93 *Use the following phrase to start a piece of writing: Sitting in the empty room he/she...*

Read back over what you've written. Did you find that you got stuck with some rather long, introspective first sentences? If this was a problem, try again, but this time start with the simpler: *He/She looked, gazed, pushed* or *sat...*

Kate Atkinson, writer of *Case Histories* and three other novels about private detective Jackson Brodie, is an expert at letting the reader see what characters are thinking. She often follows a different character in each successive chapter, taking us into a new worldview and set of experiences every time.

SURPRISE

Revealing surprising things about yourself in your writing

Lots of writers use surprise in their plotting. They create twists halfway through their stories. (Sarah Waters is wonderful at this. The twist halfway through her novel *Fingersmith* made me gasp out loud in Starbucks.) They create cliffhangers at chapter ends. Many of Roald Dahl's short stories finish on the biggest twist of all.

But you can create surprise in characterisation too. A totally predictable character is no fun to read. A character who startles sets new parts of the plot in motion.

To help you consider this, we're going to work on the character you know best of all – yourself.

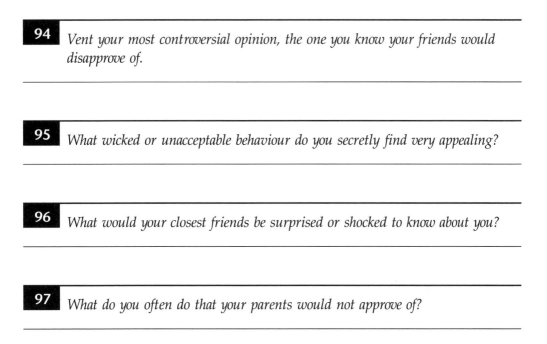

94 *Vent your most controversial opinion, the one you know your friends would disapprove of.*

95 *What wicked or unacceptable behaviour do you secretly find very appealing?*

96 *What would your closest friends be surprised or shocked to know about you?*

97 *What do you often do that your parents would not approve of?*

Surprise is a very useful quality to cultivate in your writing. If everything in there is something the reader expects, you won't hold their attention for long. If you can surprise them, without either confusing them or making them think, 'But X would **never** do that!' then you'll keep them hooked to the last page.

TWO HEADERS 1

Writing scenes for pairs of characters

Romeo and Juliet. Holmes and Watson. Harry Potter and Voldemort. Arthur and Merlin. Two people can be lovers, enemies, best friends, mentor and disciple, or any number of other things to each other. The conversation between them is always going to be fascinating.

These tasks will get you writing situations using just two characters. You might want to try them as short playscripts, with names in the margin, lots of dialogue and minimal stage directions. You might want to write them as stories, or scenes from stories.

98 *Write about a blind date. Two people have been set up by a mutual friend. How well do they get on?*

99 *Write about a doctor–patient consultation. What is the patient worried about? Can the doctor reassure them?*

Two Headers 1

100 *A troubled or argumentative caller phones in to a late-night radio show. Is the DJ soothing, or confrontational?*

101 *Two characters are trying to have an important conversation, but they keep being interrupted. What are they talking about? Who or what interrupts them?*

Plays, of course, are made of dialogue. It moves everything on stage forwards. Most stories too, and all novels, need dialogue to stop them feeling flat and dead. Fiction with no dialogue is only ever a summary of itself.

You'll get another chance to work on some more two headers later in this book. In the meantime, think about how you use such dialogue to reveal characters and their relationships and to move your plots forward.

HAIKU

Creating tiny, perfect poems following clear guidelines on form

Haiku is a three-line form of poetry that originated in Japan. Haiku are often 'noticing' poems – they act as a tiny record of something seen, often something natural and seasonal.

The modern Scottish writer Alan Spence is an expert in haiku. Here's a very sensory one:

> *sunlight through stained glass*
> *fragrance of oranges*
> *the sound of a bell*

This one haunted me for a long time:

> *the tiny light flashes*
> *a message on the machine*
> *he died last night*

Did he mean that there was a message from one friend telling him that another had died? Or did he mean that he could not bear to erase a message from someone who had passed away since leaving it?

The classic haiku has exactly seventeen syllables in three lines, arranged in the pattern of five, seven, five. Here's one about a most unclassical subject:

> *serious error*
> *all shortcuts have disappeared*
> *screen, mind, both are blank*

HAIKU

---

102 *Find a photograph of nature or landscape. Write a haiku describing it, sticking to seventeen syllables arranged in lines of five, seven and five syllables.*

---

103 *Write a haiku about the most memorable thing that has happened to you today.*

---

104 *Write a haiku about the weather or season you are experiencing just now.*

---

105 *Using the computer poem above as an example, try to write a haiku about the most unromantic and unpoetic subject you can think of.*

A poet friend of mine practises what she calls 'collecting a small stone' every day. She tries each day to carefully notice and remember one moment, experience or sight. Then she writes a haiku about it. Perhaps you could try this for a week or a month. It could be a creative way to start or end your day, and an interesting alternative to a diary or journal. If you'd like to read more of Alan Spence's haiku, I recommend his collections *Seasons of the Heart* and *Glasgow Zen*.

BEING SPECIFIC

Making your descriptions precise

It's always better to be precise in your language, because it makes the world you are creating seem so much more real for your reader. The people in the house opposite mine don't have a *dog*, they have a *border terrier the colour of wet sand*. My nephews didn't leave one of their *little toys* stuffed down the back of my sofa, they left a *Lego brick with one of its eight studs inexplicably broken off*. We didn't have *pizza* for tea on Monday, we had *home-made pizza with shards of pancetta cooked into the tomato sauce*.

These exercises will get you to create specific language.

106 *Choose one of these children's toys and make it more specific: scooter, doll, teddy, dolls' house, board game.*

107 *Choose one of these items of clothing and make it more specific: hat, coat, scarf, pair of jeans, boots, shirt.*

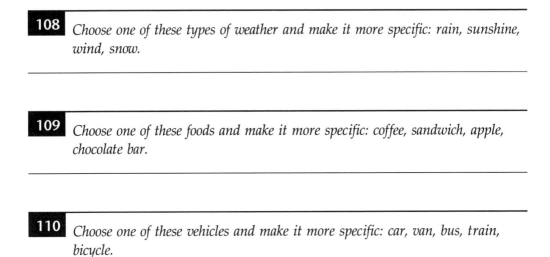

108 *Choose one of these types of weather and make it more specific: rain, sunshine, wind, snow.*

109 *Choose one of these foods and make it more specific: coffee, sandwich, apple, chocolate bar.*

110 *Choose one of these vehicles and make it more specific: car, van, bus, train, bicycle.*

What are you reading just now? As you enjoy the next chapter, look out for how the author makes objects seem real and specific.

FAMILIARITY

Reading and re-reading to find examples of good writing

When I finish reading a book, especially a paperback, I decide its fate. If I think a friend would enjoy it, I pass it on. If I'm not sure I'll re-read it, I put it in the bag for the Oxfam bookshop. If I can imagine reading it again, or looking in it to check something up, it's given its rightful place on my bookshelf.

I still have some of the books I first read in childhood. I go back to *The Wind in the Willows* again and again, particularly to the chapter about the Mole returning to his abandoned home. I revisit *The Lion, The Witch and The Wardrobe* for its promise of another world. From among my adult favourites, Jasper Fforde's *The Eyre Affair*, in which the world of books is every bit as real as ours, beguiles me every time.

If a book makes you want to read it again and again, there is something about it that can inform your own writing. Or, if a book is about a subject you know well, you can judge how well the writer handles the material.

111 *Read again a book you loved as a child. What do you still like about it now? Why do you think you adored it all those years ago?*

112 *Read a travel book – a work of literature, not a travel guide – about a place you have been to. How well did the writer bring this location to life? Did the writer's perceptions and experiences match yours?*

113 *Read the biography or autobiography of a person you think you already know a lot about. Did you feel the writer portrayed this person fairly? What did you learn that you didn't know already?*

114 *Which adult book would you say is your favourite? What is it that makes you love it so? How would you persuade a friend to read it?*

Plagiarism is theft, but imitation is the sincerest form of flattery. If a writer makes you want to read, and read again, there must be something you can learn from that.

REWRITES

Taking inspiration from other people's stories

Shakespeare adapted most of his plots from history, or from other people's plays. Then other people rewrote him: *West Side Story* is *Romeo and Juliet* with Puerto Ricans. Angela Carter turned fairy tales and legends into fabulously vivid, sensual short stories.

It's not compulsory to have original ideas, only to try to write well about them. These tasks will all get you to start with someone else's material and make it your own.

115 *Record a TV drama you know nothing about. Watch a scene with the sound off. Write the script you think the scene should have.*

116 *Create a modernised version of a famous fairy tale or nursery rhyme. What kind of 'wolves' might a red-coated girl meet nowadays? What's the twenty-first century equivalent of being swept off your feet by a charming prince? What sort of fall would a contemporary Humpty have?*

117 *Go to a jumble sale or a charity shop and buy a novel with an utterly dreadful beginning. Make a list of reasons why the opening is so terrible. What was the writer trying to do? Rewrite it to achieve this.*

118 *Try ghostwriting: get someone to tell you a story about their life. Make notes, but don't try to get it down word for word, and don't record it. Write it up later in first person, as if you are the person the story happened to.*

The best rewrite of all is the one you carry out on your own work: redrafting. Never be afraid to go back to something you've written before and try to make it better.

IRRITATIONS

Exploring what characters do when things go wrong from the start

If you've ever accused your printer of deliberately lacking ink just when you urgently need to run something off, you are a resistentialist. If you think your keys are hiding from you, you are a resistentialist. Resistentialism is the belief that inanimate objects have turned against us.

You'll find this belief in Terry Pratchett's Discworld novels, where it is called malignity. One example he gives is that garden hoses, no matter how carefully you wind them up, will unravel when you are not looking and tie your bike to your lawnmower. Discworld even has a goddess of things that get stuck in drawers.

These prompts all begin with something going wrong. You might want to let it mess up your character's day, or you might want to redeem the situation. You can show what a character is really like when you confront them with adversity, either big or small.

IRRITATIONS

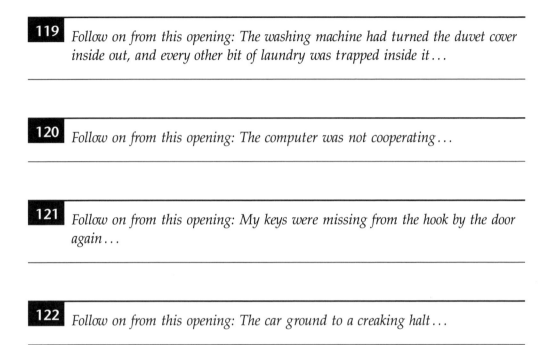

119 *Follow on from this opening: The washing machine had turned the duvet cover inside out, and every other bit of laundry was trapped inside it...*

120 *Follow on from this opening: The computer was not cooperating...*

121 *Follow on from this opening: My keys were missing from the hook by the door again...*

122 *Follow on from this opening: The car ground to a creaking halt...*

All the prompts featured mechanical or metallic objects. Perhaps it's easy to imagine something so hard and inhuman being against us.

What would happen if the soft things in life wanted to provoke us? Could you write a story where the irritating item is a cushion, or a coat? Could you craft a tale round a malicious scarf, or a mean-minded pair of slippers? Maybe it's your bath towel, not your computer, that wants to make your life a misery.

WHAT IF? 1

Using hypothetical situations to kick off stories

Some of the stories I have most enjoyed writing began with a *'What if?'* What would happen if we found out how to talk to animals, and to listen to what they were saying to us? What if vampires weren't as sexy and daring as their current media image makes them out to be? What if you found a lot of used bank notes in a bag dumped in the street?

These *'What if?'* questions will start your stories off. If you have a friend to work with, it can be a good idea to brainstorm all the possible things that might follow from this first event. Once you've got a good long list, pick the ideas you'd like to use in your writing.

---

123   *What if someone finds a business card dropped in the street and phones the number on it?*

---

124   *What if a traveller opens a briefcase that another passenger leaves on the train? What's in it?*

WHAT IF? 1

---

125 *What if a burglar opens a drawer in an antique desk? What does he find and what does he do with it?*

---

126 *What if a gardener, or a builder laying foundations, digs up something unexpected?*

When I explored my questions, I found out that nobody wanted to eat meat any more if we could speak to the animals it came from. Vampires turned out to be awfully quiet and shy, and liked working at Oxford University where they could hide in dusty college libraries. Used banknotes are very popular with students struggling with enormous debt.

What did you find out as you answered your questions?

DIFFERENCES

Creating and combining strongly contrasting characters

You are going to see 14 rows of connected words

black	grey	white
water	wine	whisky
dog	cat	snake
nightshirt	pyjamas	naked
high school	university	Ph.D.
ricotta	cheddar	stinky stilton
tweet	blog	autobiography
slim	stocky	obese
shaved	short	tresses
believer	agnostic	atheist
left	middle	right
knickers	thong	go commando
oatcake	cupcake	whole cake
bike	train	plane

127 *First, without deliberating, choose one word from each row. Circle them, or make a list.*

128 *Once again quickly, pick another word from each row. Box them, or make a second list.*

These lists now describe two characters you are going to write about. Don't feel you have to take the words too literally.

129 *Write a piece that features both characters getting along or being friends. Then have one of their differences cause a disturbance in their relationship.*

130 *Write a piece that has the characters in conflict or unsure of each other. Then use one of their differences to somehow bring them closer.*

Which seemed more likely to you? Do you believe opposites attract, or repel?

A NICE SURPRISE

Starting stories with unexpected but pleasant events

Starting a story with a surprise is a great way to intrigue your readers and draw them in. Life is full of nasty little surprises, but we'll deal with them elsewhere. For now, use these as the openings to stories that begin with an unexpected but nice event.

131 *I counted the contents of my wallet. I counted them again. I knew I'd taken £20 out of the bank earlier, so why did I now have £500?*

132 *The envelope was covered in exotic stamps from many different countries. It seemed to have been forwarded at least five times. At the bottom corner, in writing I did not recognise, were my own name and address. It smelled faintly of cinnamon.*

A Nice Surprise

---

133 *I clicked open the email. 'Congratulations!' said the message. 'You are a winner! Your prize is . . .'*

---

134 *I'm about thirty years too old to believe in Santa Claus, so I was rather surprised when he landed on the rug. It was April too. And it's a gas fire.*

Did your story stay pleasant all the way through? One of the classic descriptions of a short story is that it should put its characters through challenges and problems. If you found any of these hard to write, go back and take a look again. What would happen if the happy opening led to something darker and more complex?

Any short story probably needs no more than two surprises in it – make your fictional world any more startling and readers won't believe in it. A longer text, a play or a novel, can support far more unexpected events. Some genres, such as thrillers or detective fiction, rely on constant surprises and shocks, both for the reader and for the characters.

INSULTS

Letting rip with short but powerful language

I'm sure you've heard some of these. *He's not the sharpest tool in the box. She's a sandwich short of a picnic. He's not dealing off a full deck.* My current favourite, overheard recently, is '*I think that boy's cheese has slid right off his cracker.*'

Part of the power of these insults is that they are funny, and creative, when they are often about people who are anything but. They allow us to cut our enemies down to size with the force of our wit.

Winston Churchill was a master of the well-wrought insult. Lady Astor once said that if he were her husband, she would poison his coffee. His answer: '*Madam, if I were your husband, I should drink it!*' Another female opponent told him he was drunk. '*Bessie, you're ugly. But in the morning, I shall be sober.*' Of one enemy he said: '*He has all the virtues I dislike, and none of the vices I admire.*'

These tasks will let you sharpen the blade of your language on those you despise. If it helps, you can think of a particular person as you write. This might be someone you know personally. If you are far too nice to have rivals and enemies, you could think of a celebrity or other public figure.

135 *Create an insult that points out someone else's stupidity.*

136 *Create an insult that suggests someone's cowardice.*

137 *Create an insult that makes someone sound clumsy or disorganised.*

138 *Create an insult that points out someone's disastrous record with the opposite sex.*

These exercises have all let you practise create short and powerful language – always a useful skill. You might also find that you want to go on writing about the characters who deserve these insults, or about the characters who might say these things about someone.

AUDIENCE

Changing what you write to suit different readers

Every piece of writing has a purpose, and an audience. Nigella Lawson's books explain to cooks how they can make certain foods. A takeaway menu explains to hungry people how they can order and buy certain foods. The AA road atlas tells drivers how to get from one point to another.

We often change the way we tell stories to suit our audience. Sometimes we do this to protect the listener, sometimes to protect ourselves. We may do it because we know their interests, or because we want to make or retain a certain impression on them.

139 *Describe your weekend the way you would do if your mother asked what you'd done.*

140 *Describe your weekend the way you would do if your best friend asked what you'd done.*

---

141 *Explain the Second World War as you would do if a child asked you about it.*

---

142 *Explain British politics for someone from a country with no democratic tradition.*

You could also try describing your last holiday as if you'd been asked by a job interviewer who knows you've just come back from it; or explaining how to make an omelette to an elderly widower who's never had to cook before.

When you're writing fiction, think about the dialogue you give your characters. They will rarely say things straight; they'll nearly always fit the words they say to the person they are saying them to.

Food

Writing vividly about tastes and memories

Nigel Slater's memoir, *Toast*, contains some fantastically vivid descriptions of food. Here's what happens the first time he eats spaghetti bolognese: '*I do as Mother bids, twirling the pasta round my fork while shovelling the escaping pieces back on with my spoon. I rather like it, the feel of the softly slippery noodles, the rich sauce which is hot, salty and tastes partly of tomato, partly of Bovril.*' He's not quite so enamoured with the drum of ready-grated Parmesan cheese that he's given to sprinkle on top. '*Daddy, this cheese smells like sick.*'

His description includes not just what the food tasted and smelled like, but also the texture of the noodles, and the physical challenge of keeping them in place. Depending what you are eating, it should be possible to get in sight and even sound too. Try to use all your senses as you describe these meals.

143 *Describe the most disgusting thing you have ever eaten.*

144 *Write about the food you loved when you were ten.*

Food

145
Describe the most delicious meal you have ever eaten.

146
Write about the food that is your favourite now, or that you eat for comfort.

Because food is such a basic need, it's very tied to our emotions and personalities. I was a terribly fussy eater as a child, and more or less lived off Jacob's cream crackers, buttered, sprinkled with salt, stuck together and cut in two like a crackly sandwich. That peculiar diet tells you a lot about what kind of girl I was.

Food is also deeply connected to our families, and our relationships, because we so often eat together, and because the parents who love us cook for us. When you wrote, did you only write about the food itself, or about the people who were there with you? If you wrote only about what you ate, try one more piece in which you describe a meal with others. A family Christmas, or a dinner party, is a good place to start.

MOST AND LEAST

Using what we like, and what we don't

For the last 25 years, a survey asking Britons which profession they trust most has seen doctors come out on top. The next most trusted are teachers, judges, and the clergy. The British public do not have faith in journalists, politicians, or estate agents.

These first two tasks will get you to confound these firmly-held beliefs.

147 *Tell a story in which a character with one of the most respected jobs is actually the bad guy.*

148 *Tell a story in which a character with one of the least respected jobs is actually the good guy.*

It might interest you to know that the survey to find Britain's most trusted profession was commissioned by the Royal College of Physicians, which is, of course, the professional body of doctors. Do you still feel you trust the survey?

Most and Least

When the books blog of *The Guardian* newspaper asked readers for their favourite words, suggestions included: *defenestration* and *perihelion*. My favourite word is the much simpler *mitten*. It sounds like, and means, something small, safe and comforting.

When asked for their least favourite words, the same Guardian readers came up with *pulchritude, spatula, redacted* and *chillax*.

---

149 *Make a list of your top ten favourite words. Use at least three in a piece of writing. Try to make them seem unpleasant and disturbing.*

---

150 *Make a list of your ten most-disliked words. Use at least three in a piece of writing. Try to make them sound entrancing and beguiling.*

Did you know what all those *Guardian* readers' words meant? If not, look them up, and try to use them soon in your own writing.

ONOMATOPOEIA

Creating a lively world of sound and movement

Onomatopoeic words are ones that sound like what they mean. They are often words for noises, or for movements.

My favourite onomatopoeia is *splash*. You can absolutely hear the sound of the pebble hitting the surface of the pond in the opening *-sp-* sound, and the soft ripples of the water circling outwards in the *-sh-* at the end of the word.

Poet Matt Harvey, who was the first ever writer in residence at Wimbledon, wrote *Thwok*, a poem that describes almost an entire tennis match through onomatopoeia. Here's an extract:

> *thwackety wackety zingety ping*
> *hittety backety pingety zang*
> *wack, thwok, thwack, pok,*
> *thwikety, thwekity, thwokity, thwakity*

To enjoy the possibilities of onomatopoeia, create a poem or a piece of prose, as you feel led.

ONOMATOPOEIA

---

151   *Write about the demolition of a block of flats, using as many of these as possible:* **bang, smash, clunk, thump, tinkle, crash, clang, boom.**

---

152   *Write about a GP's day of appointments with his or her patients, using as many of these as possible:* **ping, hush, mumble, plop, burp, hiccup.**

---

153   *Write about a zoo or a farm using as many of these as possible:* **moo, oink, buzz, flutter, cuckoo, quack, squeak, meow, hiss, woof, purr, screech.**

---

154   *Write about dancing using as many of these as possible:* **swish, swirl, whirl, stomp, tap.**

Using onomatopoeia will make your written world a lively one, full of sound and movement. It will also help you to show, rather than to tell, a vital skill that we've practised elsewhere, and are about to focus on again.

SHOW, DON'T TELL 2

Returning to the basic skill that will improve everything you write

Earlier in the book you had a chance to practise this skill by rewriting the same three basic sentences in different ways.

Because this is such an important skill, we're coming back to it now.

155 *Show that a character is angry just by describing the way he/she buys three items at the supermarket.*

156 *Show that a character is afraid just by describing the way he/she starts a car and drives off.*

157 *Show that a character is worried just by describing the way he/she answers a ringing phone.*

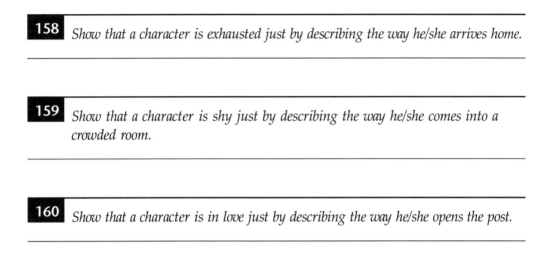

158 *Show that a character is exhausted just by describing the way he/she arrives home.*

159 *Show that a character is shy just by describing the way he/she comes into a crowded room.*

160 *Show that a character is in love just by describing the way he/she opens the post.*

The best writing always leaves at least a little tiny bit of work for the reader to do. Showing, not telling, will get you there.

THE FIRST TIME 2

Recalling more significant personal experiences to use in your writing

You've already had one opportunity to consider some of life's big firsts. These experiences stay engraved on our memories long after we've gone fuzzy on the next time, and all the times after that.

These tasks will get you to remember some more first times. What did you think, or feel? What do remember seeing, smelling, tasting, touching, or hearing? Was the experience what you had expected it would be?

---

161 *Write about the first time you visited a foreign country.*

---

162 *Write about the first time you drove a car.*

---

163 *Write about the first time you went to a football match.*

---

164 *Write about your first day at school – primary or secondary.*

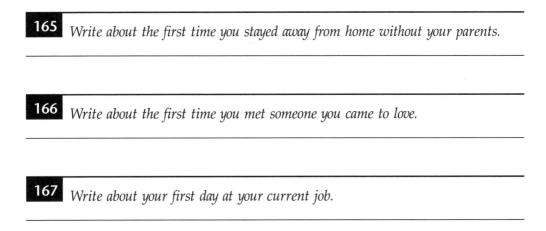

165 *Write about the first time you stayed away from home without your parents.*

166 *Write about the first time you met someone you came to love.*

167 *Write about your first day at your current job.*

What could you do with these firsts? You might give one of them to a character in a story. If so, you've got the freedom to let them experience the event a little differently. Your character could be nervous where you were confident, or successful in circumstances where you didn't do so well.

There's a Marianne Faithfull song called *The Ballad of Lucy Jordan* which is about the things the character realises she'll never do. She's only 37, but already she knows that some of life's opportunities have passed her by, or will never come her way. What will you never get to do? How do you feel about that?

Rites of Passage

Telling stories at key moments in life

There are times when life jumps the points and ends up on another track. Some of these times are very personal, but others come to most or all of us. Our societies, our families, and our churches have created rites of passage, ceremonies to mark these times. Baptisms, graduations, weddings, wakes and funerals give us a reassuring format to help us get through such moments.

168 *Tell the story of a wedding from the point of view of a guest who wishes he/she were one of the people getting married. How does your character cope?*

169 *Two school friends who haven't seen each other in years meet up at a funeral. Who died? What do they say? What happens?*

Rites of Passage

170 *Use a school or university graduation as a setting for a piece of writing. Do you want to focus on the graduate, or the proud family? Did the graduate get the result that he/she (or their family) wanted?*

171 *Use a school or university reunion as a setting for a piece of writing. Who has come? Did their life turn out the way their classmates would have expected? Do people still fit the roles they filled when they were all classmates together?*

If you'd like to watch a movie version of one of these rites of passage, *Grosse Pointe Blank* stars John Cusack as a professional assassin attending his high school reunion. For a novel version, David Nicholls's *One Day* begins with a university graduation and follows the same two characters for the next twenty years. *Four Weddings and a Funeral* packs in five rites of passage, each with a very different mood.

Which other rites of passage can you think of? How could you use one of these to inspire a piece of writing?

RECYCLED POEMS

Reworking, reusing and responding to good and bad poems

Some poems have a recognisably strong rhyme and rhythm that's just begging to be reworked.

Mary had a little lamb
A lobster, and some prunes
A piece of pie, a glass of milk
And then some macaroons
It made the naughty waiters grin
To see her order so
And when they carried Mary out
Her face was white as snow

Some poems have lines or images that haunt or beguile us, and take on a life of their own.

RECYCLED POEMS

172 *Pick a poem that has strong rhyme and rhythm. Write a parody or a new version of it, using the same structure. (You could also try 'Mary Had a Little Lamb', or maybe Wordsworth's daffodil poem, 'I Wandered Lonely as a Cloud' if you like.)*

173 *Pick a poem you love. Take one line or image from it to use in a poem or prose piece of your own.*

174 *Find a poem that you don't like. Pick one line or phrase in it that you do enjoy and use that in a piece of writing.*

175 *Find a poem that you like. Write a piece that answers it, or responds to it, or use a line from it in a poem of your own.*

If you'd like to see how poets have responded to the work of other writers, I recommend two anthologies. *Conversation Pieces*, published by Everyman's Library, and *Answering Back*, published by Picador and edited by Carol Ann Duffy both contain fascinating examples.

GIVING LIFE 1

Imagining the lives of others

Do you ever find yourself wondering what other people's lives are like? Do you think that you can guess their job, or their political beliefs from the way they order their latte? Can you tell what their marriage is like from how they chain up their bike?

The Scottish novelist Doug Johnstone says, '*To a writer, everyone else is wandering around with a sign round their neck asking, "What is it like to be me?"* ' You are going to take real people you hardly know, and turn them into believable fictions.

---

176 *Think about you someone you see often but do not really know, like a shop assistant, another member at your gym or someone who catches the same commuter train as you do. Give them a life.*

---

177 *Imagine the wife or husband of a famous historical character. What does the spouse think of their famous partner, and of their actions?*

---

178 *The Oscar-winning actor is alone in the dressing room. Show how this person thinks and feels by describing just what he/she does.*

179 *Pick a minor character from a current news story: the teenage son of the disgraced cabinet minister; the witness to the crime; the footballer left on the bench on the night of the vital cup game. Write their version of the story.*

Carol Ann Duffy's poetry collection *The World's Wife* does this many times over. If you'd like to know what Mrs Dickens thinks of the revolutionary evolutionist, or how Frau Freud feels about her husband, it's all in there.

FLASHBACKS 2

Working out what brought your characters to a certain point

The 2011 film version of *Jane Eyre*, staring Mia Wasikowska and Michael Fassbender, starts dramatically. We see Jane slip out of Rochester's Thornfield Hall and flee across the moors, eventually collapsing, exhausted, at the door of a windswept parsonage. From there the film flashes back to Jane's childhood, her unhappy schooling, and her time at Thornfield. We don't catch up with that opening until about three quarters of the way through the movie, by which time we understand her desperate escape.

You're going to see four dramatic openings. Write the flashback that tells your reader how the character ended up in this tricky position.

180 *I couldn't believe my bad luck. The time machine had transported me right into the middle of a battlefield, and a man with a sword was pelting towards me.*

181 *The first creature moved remarkably fast for something hopping on one leg. The second, scuttling along on three legs, was even quicker.*

182 *As I walked towards the spot where I thought the mysterious craft had landed, the ground gave way beneath me.*

183 *Teleportation is uncomfortable at the best of times. Our machine is so old and unreliable that when we materialised I had one of X's legs where my arm should have been, and she/he had my arm where his/her leg should be.*

You may have noticed that all these openings had a distinct science fiction slant to them, though I didn't mention that at the start. Did you perhaps think that might not be your genre? How did you get on with them?

SPIES

Spying on the people around you to create characters and plots

I saw him in the cinema queue, a little boy in Spiderman shorts and a Superman T-shirt, jumping around beside his parents. Then I noticed that his left leg was hard, shiny, and a bit too much the colour of an Elastoplast – a prosthetic leg. It was covered in scratches and bashes. He clearly did a lot of running and jumping, probably wearing his heroic shorts, for the leg to be so damaged. He obviously had no reservations about being like this. He knew he was a superhero.

These tasks will send you off to collect memorable real people you can use in your writing.

You could go to:

- a coffee shop;
- a checkout queue;
- a bus (stop);
- a gig;
- a club or bar;
- a busy changing room;
- where else...?

You can spy by:

- just listening quietly and remembering;
- pretending to read but really listening in;
- pretending to listen to your iPod but not actually having it switched on;
- taking notes when it looks like you're working.

The following exercises are examples of things you might come back with:

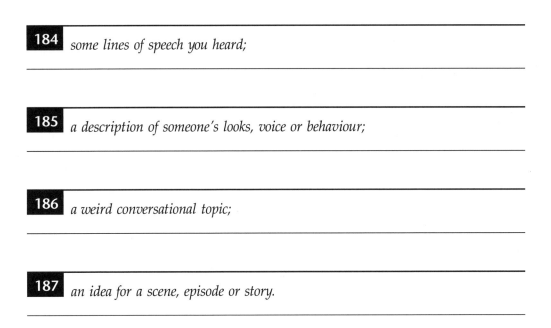

184 *some lines of speech you heard;*

185 *a description of someone's looks, voice or behaviour;*

186 *a weird conversational topic;*

187 *an idea for a scene, episode or story.*

Now decide what to do with your discoveries. Will you use exactly what you heard or saw, or will they be a wider inspiration? Do you want to give a story to a character you saw, or give their words to someone else you have created?

LOVELY LISTS 2

Using more lists to make you see things differently

Around 250 years ago, Christopher Smart created a wonderful poem that is just a huge list of all the reasons why he was fascinated by his cat, Jeoffry. He tells us how his cat *'rolls upon prank'* and that *'he counteracts the powers of darkness by his electrical skin and glaring eyes'*. He describes Jeoffry *'brisking about the life'* and, in my favourite line, says his pet, *'can spraggle upon waggle at the word of command'*. At every stage of the list, Smart's powers of observation and his love of language are vividly clear.

Here are four more chances to make lists. Spend a few minutes on each one. Let your imagination, and your love of language, lead you. Try to write something nobody else would think of. Be delightfully oblique. What dissolves? Inhibitions after a few drinks. What gets kept in the attic? A mad first wife. What is found on the shoreline? Forgotten flip flops from the furthest far-flung oceans.

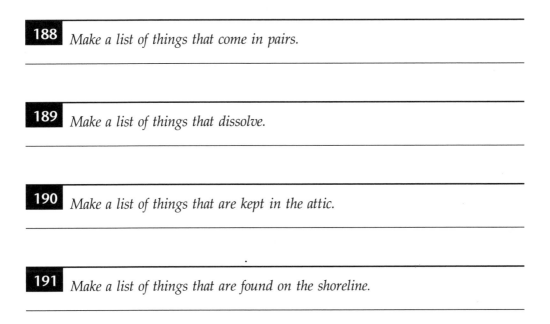

188 *Make a list of things that come in pairs.*

189 *Make a list of things that dissolve.*

190 *Make a list of things that are kept in the attic.*

191 *Make a list of things that are found on the shoreline.*

If you'd like to explore someone else's list, listen to, or look up the lyrics of, the song *'Palaces of Montezuma'* by Nick Cave's band Grinderman. It's a marvellous and inventive catalogue of all the things the narrator wants to give as gifts to his beloved.

You'll find one more chance to make curious lists later in the book.

LYRICS

Taking inspiration from the words of songs

Not all great songs have great lyrics. *She Loves You* by the Beatles is hardly going to win any creative writing prizes, no matter how much fun it is to sing along to. But some lyrics are clever and thoughtful, and there are plenty of people who'll try to convince you that Bob Dylan is a poet. Let's look at how lyrics can inspire your writing.

192 *Put some headphones on and listen until you find a line in a song that you really like. Use it as the opening for a story.*

193 *Put some headphones on and listen until you find a line in a song that appeals to you. Write a piece that ends with that lyric.*

LYRICS

194 *Put some headphones on and listen until you find a line in a song that grabs your attention. Write a story or scene where that lyric becomes a line of dialogue for one of the characters.*

195 *Put some headphones on and listen until you find a lyric that you really like. Write a story that uses this line as its title.*

If you want one more fun task to try, pick a lyric and try to bury it in the middle of a longer piece you are writing. Does anybody notice it isn't yours? In every case, you might find that your chosen line has done something very different in your writing to what it originally did in the song.

My favourite American band, The Decemberists, write the most fascinating lyrics. In their songs you'll find words like *ravine, parapet, petticoats, flue, catacombs, troughs, magenta, rend, parodies, palanquin, concubine and pachyderm.* None of these words is exactly common in everyday English, yet The Decemberists use every one perfectly in their songs, so that these striking terms become immediately the best word they could possibly have used at that point.

FRIENDS AND ENEMIES

Letting memories of friendship inspire characters and stories

'*Keep your friends close and your enemies even closer,*' says Al Pacino's character Michael Corleone in *The Godfather*. The world of books is full of friends and enemies: Harry Potter has Ron and Hermione, Peter Pan has Captain Hook. Sometimes the same person is a friend and an enemy. Macbeth trusts Banquo, then turns on him and has him killed. Othello trusts Iago, who is secretly trying to destroy him.

Friendship, and its opposite, are engines that drive many plots.

---

196 *Who was your best friend as a child? What experiences did you have together? What is the state of that friendship now?*

---

197 *Who was your worst childhood enemy? What did you do to make your enemy suffer? What did your enemy do to you?*

---

198 *Who do you see every day that you'd be happy not to see for a few weeks? Why? Who have you not seen for a few weeks that you'd love to see right now? Why?*

199 *Which friend is most unlike you? Describe this person. What is it that draws you together?*

These tasks have made you write from personal experience. Look back at what you've written. Could any of it become an inspiration for fiction? Could one of the friends you've written about be turned into a character?

SENSES 2

Exploring each sense deeply and thoughtfully

Earlier in the book you had an opportunity to use all your senses in writing about a food. Many of the other exercises have also reminded you to bring all the senses into what you write.

These exercises will get you to focus deeply on one sense at a time.

200 *Close your eyes in an empty, quiet room and listen for a minute. Write about what you hear.*

201 *Go into a dark room and wait until your eyes adjust. Describe what you see.*

202 *Stand utterly still for a minute. Describe what you feel.*

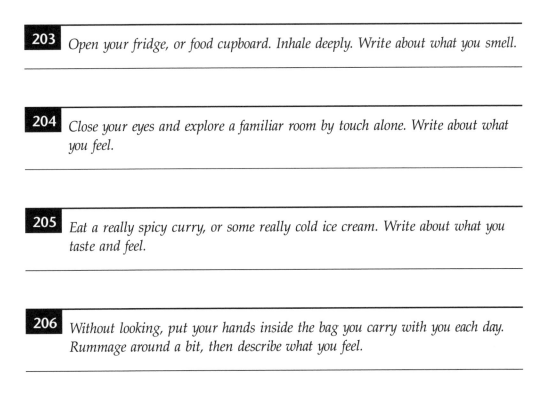

203 *Open your fridge, or food cupboard. Inhale deeply. Write about what you smell.*

204 *Close your eyes and explore a familiar room by touch alone. Write about what you feel.*

205 *Eat a really spicy curry, or some really cold ice cream. Write about what you taste and feel.*

206 *Without looking, put your hands inside the bag you carry with you each day. Rummage around a bit, then describe what you feel.*

Keep remembering in your writing, a real world is so much more than what you see.

Descriptions 2

Writing descriptions that imply an opinion

Earlier in this book you had the opportunity to write what we might call objective descriptions, telling us what something is just plainly like. But we are rarely quite so unbiased. If you like someone, you might call her *curvaceous*, but if you couldn't stand her, you'd probably say she was *fat*. Your friend might be *tipsy*, your enemy, *drunk*. The same person might be *sociable* or *attention-seeking*, depending on who says so.

These tasks will get you writing descriptions that have a bit of a spin to them. You are not just trying to say what something is actually like, you are trying to make the reader feel the way you feel about this object.

Remember to be sparing with adjectives and adverbs, and to try to use all your senses into your descriptions.

207 *Look in the bag you most often carry with you. Find an object – maybe one you had forgotten was in there. Describe this as if you found it deeply puzzling and baffling.*

DESCRIPTIONS 2

208 *In the TV series* Outnumbered, *the frighteningly bright nine-year-old Karen said, 'Black's the colour of beetles and school shoes and Miss Barrington's enormous eyebrows.' You can tell from her choice of items that she does not like this colour. Choose a colour you dislike. Make a Karen-like list of unpleasant things that are that colour.*

209 *Pick an expensive item that you've owned for a long time – maybe your car or an electric or electronic object. Describe it in a way that would convince someone to buy you a new one.*

One way to build a character's point of view is to let us see the world, and what's in it, the way the character does, with all their bias and subjectivity.

INTROSPECTIVE

Considering yourself and your hopes and wishes

I went hot air ballooning once. We glided totally silently above the Scottish Borders very early on a July Sunday morning. The sun was just coming up over the hills and every twig and blade of grass had its own stark little shadow. If I never get the chance to fly like this again, a little part of my heart will die.

I wish I'd never bought a wedding dress. I loved my wedding, and I'm still happily married many, many years later, but dressing up, and wasting money, are both really not me. I wish I'd hired a frock just for the day, or worn something that I could wear again.

I've never learned to type properly. Everything I write is full of red underlinings as Microsoft Word despairs of my inaccuracies. My work takes twice as long as it ought to because I have to keep correcting my mistakes. If I could only touch-type, I'd be a far more efficient author.

Use these starters to consider yourself.

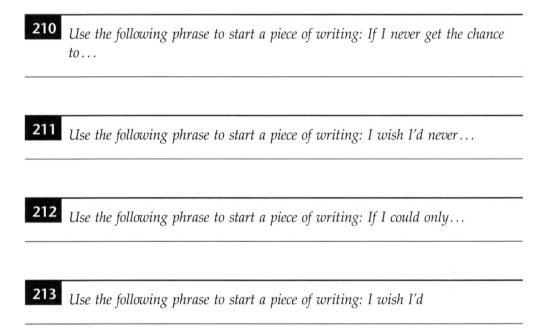

210 *Use the following phrase to start a piece of writing: If I never get the chance to . . .*

211 *Use the following phrase to start a piece of writing: I wish I'd never . . .*

212 *Use the following phrase to start a piece of writing: If I could only . . .*

213 *Use the following phrase to start a piece of writing: I wish I'd*

Look back over your work. You could use some of this as inspiration for further writing. What would happen if a character tried to fulfil one of your desires, or to avoid one of your regrets?

You may not need to write more now. Instead, it may be the right time to achieve one of these wishes, or make right a disappointment. You are the author of your life, not just of your stories.

WAYS OF TELLING

Trying unusual styles and formats for fiction

Many early novels were told at least partly in letter form. Mary Shelley's *Frankenstein*, written in 1818, is told as a series of letters from a sea captain who meets the dying Victor Frankenstein and records his story. Bram Stoker's *Dracula*, published in 1897, is compiled from letters, diary entries, newspaper clippings, telegrams, doctor's notes and ship's logs. Stoker even deploys typed-up transcripts of speech that had been dictated onto a very early form of recording machine called a phonograph.

These writers were using the means of telling that seemed available to them at the time. Our modern, technological age keeps creating new forms of text that Shelley and Stoker could never have dreamed of.

214 *Tell a story only in email messages.*

215 *Tell a story only in text messages.*

---

216 *Tell a story only in mobile phone conversations.*

---

217 *Tell a story only in tweets – messages of just 140 characters including spaces.*

These technological devices can sometimes get you out of a tight spot. I was writing a story that followed the point of view of one particular character, when I realised that the next, and crucial, part of the plot was going to involve events she would never be able to see. How to get them in then? I had her finding out about them in a series of emails from another character who did know what was happening elsewhere.

Telling an entire text in just one of these forms might have felt rather unnatural. But, don't be afraid of using a little bit of something different in your writing.

CONFLICT

Creating scenes with characters who cannot agree

The Scottish novelist Doug Johnstone says: *'Nobody wants to read about nice people doing nice things to each other for three hundred pages.'* The life we all want to live is the life none of us want to read about. Fiction needs conflict to move it forward.

But what is conflict? *Father Ted* and *IT Crowd* writer Graham Linehan says: *'You learn very quickly that there are ways of writing conflict that are a bit more subtle. If you're a good writer, you don't have everybody shouting in every scene. Conflict means a mother places something here and then when she leaves, the daughter moves it back. That's conflict. It doesn't have to be two people screaming at each other in a room.'* Linehan says that conflict is not, *'get people in, put them in the red corner and the blue corner, and make them fight'.*

The following tasks will give you the chance to explore more subtle ways of showing conflict. Each asks you to write a scene: you can do this as a playscript, or as a short fictional narrative. Whichever option you choose you will need a lot of dialogue, but remember what Linehan says about the power of tiny actions too.

It's up to you to decide if both parties are equally to blame for the conflict, or if one is more antagonistic than the other.

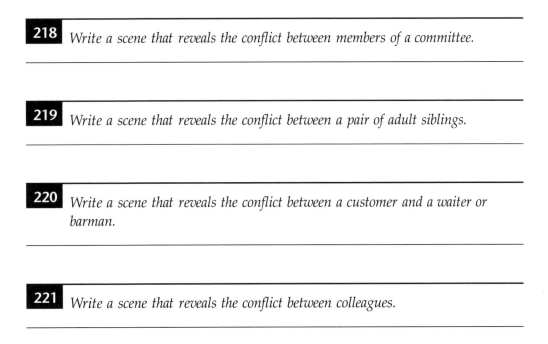

218 *Write a scene that reveals the conflict between members of a committee.*

219 *Write a scene that reveals the conflict between a pair of adult siblings.*

220 *Write a scene that reveals the conflict between a customer and a waiter or barman.*

221 *Write a scene that reveals the conflict between colleagues.*

Read back over your work. Could one of your scripts become a narrative? Would something you told as narrative work better as a script?

PICTURE PEOPLE 2

Using more photographs to help you create characters

If you wanted to know what I was like, you could get a very good notion by watching me wash the dishes. There's a little utility room just off my kitchen, and until I have time to get to work I very neatly tuck everything in there round the corner, out of sight. I stack the crockery in neat piles, and I put the cutlery, sticky end up, in the biggest of the several dirty mugs.

Then I set to. I scrape the coffee grounds into the bin and rinse the pot under the tap as I run a basin of very hot water. I start with the glasses, setting them rim down on the drainer, then move on to the mugs. Crockery comes next, followed by cutlery. I have a special drainer for this: knives, forks, spoons and teaspoons each have their own unique slot. Finally I scrub the serving dishes, baking trays and pans. I never stop until everything is spotless. Then I wipe down the kitchen worktops and the dining table.

I explained this process to my students and asked them how they would describe me. *'Meticulous,'* said one girl, kindly. I might have said uptight or obsessive. Some people might call me controlling.

For these exercises you should start by finding some photos in newspapers or magazines of people you think look interesting. Don't pick anyone you recognise – you don't want any preconceived ideas in your head.

You're going to write in third person (using he/she), and in detail, to describe your character doing a simple task. The way you describe the character and his or her actions should reveal as much as possible about what this person is like. Use as little dialogue as possible – none if you can.

222 *Write a piece in which your character is waiting to be called in for a job interview.*

223 *Describe this person trying to get a young child to go to bed.*

224 *Write a piece in which your character is packing for a week's foreign holiday.*

225 *Describe this person making a journey on a very crowded train or bus.*

This is a technique you can use again and again in your writing. Actions always speak louder than words, and will help you to show without telling.

HELL IS THE OTHERS

Opening your stories with detestable characters

There are some people we love, and some we just can't stand. Worst of all, sometimes we find we just can't stand the people we do, or should, love.

These prompts are all about the moments when we find others impossibly frustrating. Use each one as an inspiration for your own writing, or as the opening for a piece.

---

226 *After many years of staring at him, I realised it was his ridiculous beard I hated most. That and his pony tail, his bald spot, and his terrible gold hoop earring.*

---

227 *Since I had only married him for his money, I was rather upset to discover his company had gone bust while we were in the Seychelles on honeymoon.*

---

228 *I was appalled. Was she really going to wear that to the party?*

---

229 *Simon from IT had always seemed so quiet. We all tried very hard not to stare when he came into work one morning with two black eyes, a bandaged ear, and his hair dyed green.*

Sometimes frustration can be more fun than contentment. Did you surprise yourself by finding out that it can be easier to write about someone you hate than about someone you love?

The novels of Charles Dickens are full of characters who are written to irritate, like the self-made industrialist Mr Bounderby in *Hard Times*, or the social-climbing grocer Pumblechook in *Great Expectations*. Some other characters seem to annoy readers when that's probably not what the author intended: for every reader who loves J D Salinger's Holden Caulfield there's another who finds him self-indulgent.

METAPHORS

Making abstract ideas real and concrete through metaphor

Here's an extract from a poem called *'Happiness'*, by the American writer Jane Kenyon.

Happiness is the uncle you never
knew about, who flies a single-engine plane
onto the grassy landing strip, hitchhikes
into town, and enquires at every door
until he finds you asleep mid-afternoon
as you so often are during the unmerciful hours of your despair

Notice that what she is doing is constructing a metaphor that defines what happiness is and how it works. She is not saying an uncle who is like this and does this would make us happy; she is saying that one way to see what happiness is like and how it sometimes surprises us is to picture this sort of uncle.

After I read the Kenyon poem, I tried creating my own metaphor for autumn.

Autumn is a woman in her fifties who,
just at the point where it looks
as if all of that might be over,
discovers an entirely new way to be beautiful
and becomes the best herself of all.

Both of these poems, Kenyon's good one and my own modest effort, take something abstract and try to make it more solid and real through metaphor. You're going to try something similar. Write in poetry, or prose, as you wish.

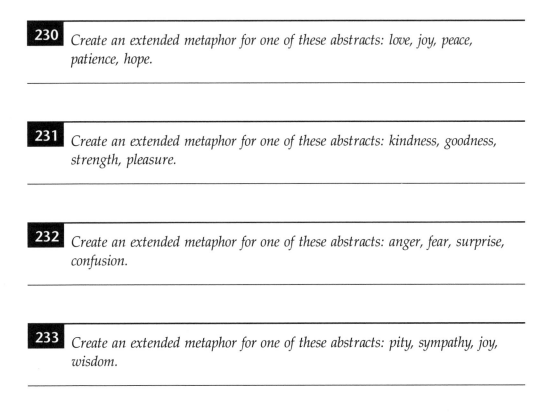

230 *Create an extended metaphor for one of these abstracts: love, joy, peace, patience, hope.*

231 *Create an extended metaphor for one of these abstracts: kindness, goodness, strength, pleasure.*

232 *Create an extended metaphor for one of these abstracts: anger, fear, surprise, confusion.*

233 *Create an extended metaphor for one of these abstracts: pity, sympathy, joy, wisdom.*

Be careful with abstracts. They can feel important but actually be vague or just plain pretentious. This exercise has let you make them concrete. Depending on what you are writing, you can also make abstracts come to life through action, interaction or dialogue.

If you'd like to read the rest of the Jane Kenyon poem, you'll find it in a collection of her work *Let Evening Come*, published by Bloodaxe.

INFLUENCE

Reflecting on the influences that have shaped your life

I grew up in a small village near Aberdeen. I'd probably have quite happily gone to Aberdeen University, and travelled back and forward from home every day on the bus, if it hadn't been for the influence of two of my teachers. When we were in our final year of school, they took eight of us to the Edinburgh Festival. As well as all the amazing art and culture, we stayed in the university hall of residence and played at being students. A year later I came to study in Edinburgh. The opportunity they gave me, and their advice that leaving home is a big part of growing up, changed my life.

234 *Write about a friend who has been a good influence on you, or a bad one.*

235 *Write about a teacher who was a good influence on you, or a bad one.*

236 *Write about a celebrity or a famous historical figure who has been a good influence on you, or a bad one.*

237 *Write about a family member who has been a good influence on you, or a bad one.*

You could take one of these influences and use it in a story. What happens if a character tries to resist a good influence, or struggles to shake off a bad one?

Of course it is not just people who influence us. You, or your characters, can be shaped by many other factors too. Health, social class, family background, events (both happy and traumatic), religion and education all shape who are and who we become. How have some of these figured in your own life? How could you use them in the lives of your characters?

What If? 2

Using more hypothetical situations to kick off stories

Some of the stories I have most enjoyed writing began with a 'What if?' What if the mythological gods all had a favourite pub? What if Cinderella's marriage was the end of the fairy tale but not the end of the story? What if scientists cracked the mystery of time travel?

These 'What if?' questions will start your stories off. If you have a friend to work with, it can be a good idea to brainstorm all the possible things that might follow from this first event. Once you've got a good long list, pick the ideas you'd like to use in your writing.

---

238 *What if someone who doesn't believe in the supernatural has an inexplicable experience?*

---

239 *What would happen if there were a 24-hour power cut?*

What If? 2

240　*What if someone wakes up from a coma, and the person they expect to see at their bedside isn't there?*

241　*What if the lift breaks down between floors? Who is in there and what happens?*

When I explored my questions, I found out that the legendary gods are startlingly human and badly-behaved. Cinderella and her prince soon ended up in marriage guidance and she wasn't the sweet girl you might hope her to be. Time travel, it turns out, severely shortens your life.

What did you find out as you answered your questions?

TRY READING THIS

Considering how your reading can shape and inform your writing

With over 200,000 books published in Britain each year, how are you ever going to find time to read the good stuff? In truth, most of us work out what we like to read, and then read more of the same. This is understandable, because we don't want to waste our precious time and money, but it's sad too. Think of all the potentially wonderful books out there that you might be missing.

I make a list each year of all the books I read. The ones that I remember best at the end of the year are often the ones that surprised me most, or challenged me most, when I read them.

242 *Pick a book by an author whose work you would never normally read. Why would you usually avoid this person's work? What did you end up liking about it?*

243 *Read a book a friend hated and try to find something to like in it.*

| 244 | *Pick a book from a genre you would never usually read. If you're a man, try some shiny-covered chick lit. If you're a sober lover of history and biography, try some fantasy or sci-fi. What can you learn from this that you could use in your own writing?* |

| 245 | *Read something which has been translated into English from another language, or a book written in a much earlier historical period. What was beautiful about the language? What seemed different about this writer's way of thinking or seeing?* |

Also, what you read will shape what you write. Your reading will show you what works and what doesn't. If you don't read widely, you won't have all the experience you need as a writer.

PHOTOGRAPHS

Letting pictures provoke words

When I was a child in the 1970s, you had to supply your own spud: Mr Potato Head did not come with the plastic body familiar to the *Toy Story* generation. One of the most memorable Cooper family photographs shows me holding up what happens if you leave your creation in the toy cupboard for a week or two. My beastie had sprouted hideous leggy growths. Another memorable picture demonstrates the unwisdom of dressing all your children in the same crimplene dress. My blonde baby sister looks cute, my curly haired younger sister looks like a beautiful boy, and I exist only to prove that ginger kids should never wear orange.

---

246 *Search out a photo you haven't seen for years. Write about the memories it brings back.*

---

247 *Choose a photo of a landscape. Write to describe this place as it might change over the course of a day. Include at least one change of weather in the piece.*

PHOTOGRAPHS

248 *Find a really bad photograph and use it to inspire a good piece of writing.*

249 *Look for a photo of a celebrity wedding in a gossip magazine. Examine the couple's body language. Write about what happens after the guests have left and the party is over.*

I often tear images from magazines and newspapers as I read them. You could do the same. Get rid of any captions so nobody else is telling you what to think. Keep the pictures in a safe place. If you need inspiration one day, pick one out at random and see what it suggests to you.

Changing Person

Switching between first and third person to see what's most effective

One decision about your fiction is whether to tell it in the first person, using *I*, or the third person, using *he* or *she*. (Second person narration, using *you*, is unusual, hard to write at length, and can feel quite odd to read.)

First person draws your readers in because they feel as if the character is talking directly to them. J D Salinger's *The Catcher In The Rye* or Harper Lee's *To Kill A Mockingbird* are two famous examples of this. Using this kind of narration does bring you challenges. You can only tell us what your character knows, sees, or experiences, and this places some restrictions on you.

Third person gives you far more freedom. You can use language that the characters themselves might not know. You can take us into the point of view of non-speaking characters: a refugee, a stroke victim, a prisoner exercising his right to silence. You can control what your readers think about the characters. Some Victorian writers, notably Dickens and George Eliot, used a truly omniscient third person, seeing into every character's mind and knowing everything about them.

CHANGING PERSON

250 *Find a piece of fiction that has been written in first person. Rewrite the first few paragraphs in third person. How is this better? What have you gained or improved? How is this worse? What have you lost?*

251 *Find a piece of fiction that has been written in third person. Rewrite the first few paragraphs in first person. How is this better? What have you gained or improved? How is this worse? What have you lost?*

If you're trying to write something that isn't working, one way to shake it up might be to change your narration from first to third person, or vice versa.

GOOGLISM

Searching the web for striking phrases

This is a stimulus task for making up poetry. It relies on one of the Google family of websites called googlism. The web address of this site is

www.googlism.com

When you look up this site you will find a search box on the front page. Enter a simple word in the box and click to search. You will get a huge list of phrases that begin with your chosen word followed by, *'is'*.

For example, if you look up the word *'poetry'* you will get expressions such as:

poetry is passion
poetry is for real people
poetry is a force
poetry is verbal compression
poetry is powerful

When a friend had a big special birthday I looked up lots of *'forty is...'* expressions and picked out some of the most striking to make a poem for her birthday card.

You're going to use this website to find material for your writing. Don't just pull a list of lines off the site and call them a poem. Instead use the lines as inspirations for your own work, reshaping them as you think best.

252 *Choose a particular age, or a certain stage of life, and use the googlism site to find striking phrases about it. Use these to inspire your own piece of writing.*

253 *Use the googlism site to find striking phrases about one of these: writing, music, painting, photography. Use these to inspire your own piece of writing.*

254 *Choose a particular sport, hobby or pastime, and use the googlism site to find striking phrases about it. Use these to inspire your own piece of writing.*

255 *Choose a particular month, or day of the week, and use the googlism site to find striking phrases about it. Use these to inspire your own piece of writing.*

Remember, it's what you do with the language of these phrases, and how you reshape them to make your own writing, that really matters here.

Parent and Child 2

Writing scenes between adults and their offspring

One of my favourite short stories is *Hansel* from Garrison Keillor's collection *Leaving Home*. It paints a touching picture of a father's relationship with his children.

> *You can see he loves them and loves it when they hang on him, and now, just as they're getting a little too wild and tired and about to break into tears, he collects them in his arms and they all lie back in a heap in the messy messy living room, and he will now tell them a story... The kids curl up close to their dad lying on his back, and before he can start the story, everyone has to get very quiet ... you can see how stories have been useful to parents over the years.*

These tasks will give you another opportunity to write about the relationships between parents and their children of all ages. Decide whether you want to tackle these as scripts, or as narratives. You might feel each one deserves a slightly different approach.

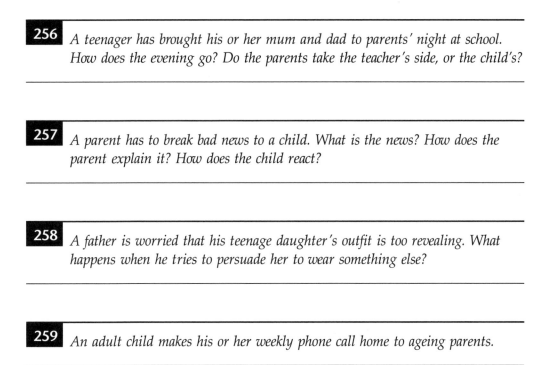

256 *A teenager has brought his or her mum and dad to parents' night at school. How does the evening go? Do the parents take the teacher's side, or the child's?*

257 *A parent has to break bad news to a child. What is the news? How does the parent explain it? How does the child react?*

258 *A father is worried that his teenage daughter's outfit is too revealing. What happens when he tries to persuade her to wear something else?*

259 *An adult child makes his or her weekly phone call home to ageing parents.*

Read back over your work. Did you find it easier to write the parents' side, or the children's? How much did your own memories or experiences support, or find their way into, what you wrote?

THE COLUMNIST

Sharing strong and original opinions about what's in the news

I'm listening to the news as I write this. The bosses of Britain's top 100 companies have enjoyed a record average 49% pay rise in the last year, while most ordinary wages struggle to keep up with inflation. St Paul's Cathedral has been closed for nearly a week because of anti-capitalist protestors camped outside. A gruesome murder trial has just come to an end. The law of succession has been changed so that a baby girl could be first in line to the British throne. Earth's seven billionth inhabitant will be born on Monday.

There's lots of meat in all of this for newspaper columnists to get their teeth into.

---

260 *Read a selection of columnists from different papers who take different approaches to the same news story. Mixing* The Sun, The Telegraph, The Guardian *and* The Daily Mail *should give you a good selection. What is each writer's main point? What supporting ideas or details do they use to back that point up? What techniques do they use to try to make their arguments convincing?*

---

261 *Now write your own column on this subject. Try to find something to say that none of the other writers have said. Think about the techniques you found in the other writers' work, and use any that will be helpful.*

---

262 *Wait a few days before choosing a different news story. Write a column about this issue. In your writing you must passionately make and argue a point that you actually don't believe in at all.*

Was it hard to defend a position you didn't agree with? Or was it liberating? Did it let you concentrate on the power of your words? Was it fun stepping outside of your usual beliefs? Really skilled writers can make words do anything for them.

POSSESSIONS

Showing what characters are like through what they choose to own

If you wanted to know what kind of person I am, you'd only have to look at my bookcases. All the books are in strict alphabetical order, according to the author's surname. What's more, these books are neatly organised by type – literary fiction, genre fiction, travel, history, poetry, biography and so on. If you think that seems normal, take a look at my spice rack, where 25 different jars of exotic flavour are also in alphabetical order. You don't need to meet me to assess my character.

263 *Write a description of a character's desk, in a way that shows what that character is like without him or her even being there.*

264 *Write a description of a fridge and its contents, in such a way that it reveals the character of its unseen owner.*

---

265 *Write a description of the contents of a character's briefcase, backpack or handbag, in a way that shows what that character is like without him or her even being there.*

---

266 *Write a description of a garage, in such a way that it reveals the character of its unseen owner.*

Which other places can you think of that reveal character? A bathroom cabinet? A shopping basket? A make-up bag? Did you base all the exercises above on the same character? Why not try creating a very different person and describing the objects in his or her life too?

FLASHBACKS 3

Working out what brought more characters to a certain point

The films known as prequels exist to explain how the events of other films made earlier, but set later, arose. George Lucas's second *Star Wars* trilogy explains how Anakin Skywalker became Darth Vader. *X Men: First Class* tells us how Magneto and Xavier became enemies, and how the mutants began to use their powers. *Rise of the Planet of the Apes* shows how the world that Charlton Heston crash lands on in the 1968 movie came into being. Some situations just beg to be explained.

You're going to see four dramatic openings. Write the flashback that tells your reader how the character ended up in this tricky position.

267 *Nuns have always reminded me of penguins, and I've never been sure about them, but with my back against the wall and no more ammo in my weapon I was very glad to see those two now.*

268 *It wasn't until we reached the summit, gasping for air, that I realised we had forgotten to bring the flag.*

269 *I took a deep breath and plunged into the icy water, striking out towards the struggling puppy/child.*

270 *Just as I breathed a sigh of relief at getting through the white water rapids, our raft overturned anyway.*

This time all the openings had a distinct action adventure slant to them, though once again I didn't mention that at the start. Did you perhaps think that might not be your genre? How did you get on with them? Could you carry any of the stories right through to its end?

There will be one more opportunity to create flashbacks later in the book.

SPELLS

Making magic out of well-chosen words and ingredients

I'm sure you know the witches' *'Double, double, toil and trouble...'* spell from Macbeth. They create that trouble with a huge list of truly disgusting ingredients. Their cauldron contains *'poisoned entrails'*, a *'witch's mummy'*, and the finger of a baby born in a ditch and strangled at birth. The disgusting ingredients they use tell us that they are going to meddle most vilely in Macbeth's life.

As you work through these ideas, try to make the ingredients really appropriate to the magic the spell is meant to work.

271 *Write a spell to make someone fall in love.*

272 *Write a spell to resurrect the dead.*

273 *Write a spell to make someone famous.*

274 *Write a spell to make a shy person confident.*

If they're mostly just lists so far, you could try re-drafting your own spells into Shakespearian rhyme, which would mean writing in rhyming couplets (pairs of rhymed lines) and using seven syllables per line, like this:

Fillet of a fenny snake,
In the cauldron boil and bake;
Eye of newt, and toe of frog,
Wool of bat, and tongue of dog,
Adder's fork, and blind-worm's sting,
Lizard's leg, and owlet's wing

Or, if your spells rhyme already, try re-writing them as very matter of fact recipes that you might find in a cookbook. You could also try adding any special actions your sorcerer needs to carry out to make the magic potent.

TIMES AND PLACES

Using memories of place and time in your writing

My favourite Philip Larkin poem, *Afternoons*, has a strong sense of time and place. He shows us the falling leaves, just a few at that moment, signalling the end of summer and start of autumn. He lets us see that the trees stand by a children's playground, near a 1950s housing estate where every garden is filled with washing hung out to dry.

If I close my eyes, I can still bring back one place I used to visit as a child, my Auntie Nan's house. Her kitchen cupboards had ridged glass doors, and inside one cupboard she kept a jar of five pence pieces. She always gave me one when I went to visit. We never sat in the parlour, because it was for best, so my conversations with her all took place in the sunporch.

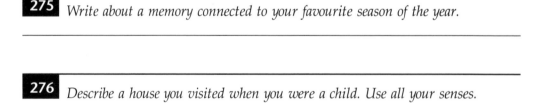

275 *Write about a memory connected to your favourite season of the year.*

276 *Describe a house you visited when you were a child. Use all your senses.*

Times and Places

---

277 *Write about your favourite time of day.*

---

278 *Write about a place you have been but never want to go back to.*

I can still conjure up the plasticky, chemical smell of the shower unit in the teachers' hostel I lived in for a year while I taught in Poland. Neuroscience tells us that our sense of smell is very closely connected to our memory. Were there fragrances and aromas in what you wrote?

Now that you have brought these places and times to life, you may wish to reuse them in a piece of fiction.

PERSUADE ME

Convincing your readers to do something astonishing

Here's part a famous speech given by Winston Churchill in June 1940, around the time of the British evacuation from Dunkirk:

Even though large tracts of Europe and many old and famous states have fallen or may fall into the grip of the Gestapo and all the odious apparatus of Nazi rule, we shall not flag or fail. We shall go on to the end. We shall fight in France, we shall fight on the seas and oceans, we shall fight with growing confidence and growing strength in the air, we shall defend our island, whatever the cost may be. We shall fight on the beaches, we shall fight on the landing grounds, we shall fight in the fields and in the streets, we shall fight in the hills; we shall never surrender, and if, which I do not for a moment believe, this island or a large part of it were subjugated and starving, then our Empire beyond the seas, armed and guarded by the British Fleet, would carry on the struggle, until, in God's good time, the new world, with all its power and might, steps forth to the rescue and the liberation of the old.

It's a brilliant example of speechmaking as it uses these highly effective persuasive techniques:

- repetition of words or phrases;
- the use of 'we', to make it seem as if the speaker and audience are in it together;
- a vision of success or achievement.

PERSUADE ME

You can also use:

- short sentences to sound dramatic;
- rhetorical questions.

Using the right mix of persuasive techniques, write a speech that will move your listeners to:

279 *regularly give part of their income to a particular charity;*

280 *do a bungee or parachute jump just for the thrill of it;*

281 *'streak' at a Premier League football match;*

282 *spend the night in a haunted house.*

Is there something you are sure you would never do? For one final challenge, write to persuade yourself to do that.

Two Headers 2

Writing more scenes for pairs of characters

One of my favourite old Hollywood movies is *The Odd Couple*. Jack Lemmon's obsessively tidy Felix moves in with Walter Matthau's slovenly Oscar and for the next hundred minutes we see them bicker, negotiate and gradually work out how their friendship might last and why their marriages haven't. Although there are other characters, including their poker buddies and a couple of English girls from the apartment upstairs, it is the pairing of Oscar and Felix, and the dialogue Neil Simon writes for them, that makes the film a classic.

These tasks will give you more opportunities to write about situations involving just two characters. You might want to try them as short playscripts, with names in the margin, lots of dialogue and minimal stage directions. You might want to write them as stories, or scenes from stories.

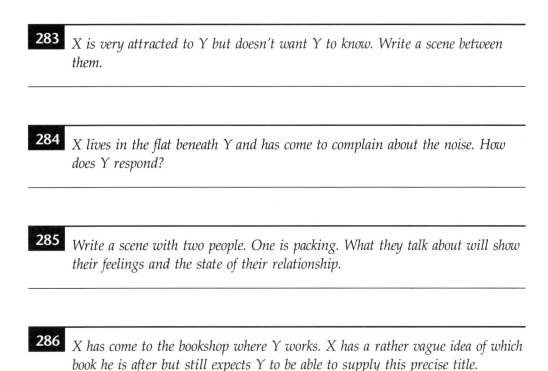

283 *X is very attracted to Y but doesn't want Y to know. Write a scene between them.*

284 *X lives in the flat beneath Y and has come to complain about the noise. How does Y respond?*

285 *Write a scene with two people. One is packing. What they talk about will show their feelings and the state of their relationship.*

286 *X has come to the bookshop where Y works. X has a rather vague idea of which book he is after but still expects Y to be able to supply this precise title.*

Read back over the scenes you've written. If you wrote them as prose, whose point of view did you follow? What would happen if you wrote from the other character's side instead? Which character came across more sympathetically in each piece? Could you rewrite the scenes to make the other character seem the more sympathetic figure?

Taboo

Avoiding the obvious words

If you only ever use the most obvious words, you will bore your reader. Why would they read on, if can they already predict what you are going to say?

Part of good writing is about using a word that is surprising, but appropriate. The reader should think, 'I wouldn't have thought of that word, but it's absolutely perfect.'

To help you with this, we're going to play a writing game that is a variation on a word game you may have played at parties.

---

287 *Two climbers are about to reach the summit of Mount Everest. Describe their triumph without using any of these words:* **cold, ice, snow, boots, struggle, top**.

---

288 *It's a busy Saturday night in the restaurant. Set a scene in the kitchen without using any of these words:* **oven, stove, order, waiter, cook, chef, burn**.

---

289 *The headmaster needs to speak to his pupils about a spate of vandalism. Write the scene without using any of these words:* **punish, angry, disappointed, teachers, pupils, toilets, graffiti, damage, suspended, expelled.**

---

290 *You're a radio reporter at a football match. Give a running commentary on the game without using any of these words:* **goal, score, kick, striker, forward, penalty.**

Read back over what you have written. There will be some places where you really do wish you could have used one of the forbidden words, because your substitute is actually a bit clunky and unnatural. Revise your work, letting yourself put back in no more than two taboo words per piece.

RESPONDING

Producing your own writing as a response to someone else's

It's easy to think of writing as a solitary activity, just you alone in a little room with a laptop or a notebook. But writers are communicators. You are writing for a reader, an audience. In these exercises you'll get a chance to think about producing writing of your own in response to something someone else has already written.

291 *Pick up a magazine you read recently. Write a letter to the editor challenging something in it that you did not agree with. Or, write a letter adding your own knowledge or experience to an article that struck a chord with you.*

292 *Go to www.amazon.co.uk and find the page for a book you've read recently. Post a review – it's incredibly easy to register to do this.*

---

293 *Find a website that lets you post reviews of films you've seen and add one. (Empire Magazine has a site that will let you do this.)*

---

294 *Go to www.blogspot-search.blogspot.com to find a blog on a subject that you're interested in. Read a number of recent posts and then submit a response.*

Just a word of warning. Especially with the blog response, and the Amazon review, there's a high chance that the original writer may read what you've said about their work. It's very easy to forget that it's another person's work you are commenting on, because you've never met them in person. How would you feel if somebody sent you the words that you are saying about them? Do be kind and constructive to your fellow writers.

If, Then

Finding poetry in the consequences that follow our actions

If she wins the Lottery, then she'll buy a big house with a huge grassy lawn. If he makes them miss the flight, then she just might have to kill him. If he can just lose enough weight, then women will fall at his feet.

One thing leads to another. These tasks will help you play with the poetry of these consequences.

---

295 *Every day for a week write a pair of phrases. Start the first phrase with, 'If...,' and the next phrase with, 'Then...' For example:*

> *If I just keep pushing,*
> *Then surely one door will open.*

or

> *If he leaves her now,*
> *Then she'll never get over it.*

or

> *If it keeps raining like this,*
> *Then she'll never go out.*

IF, THEN

296 *On the last day of the week, mix up the 'If's and 'Then's so that you get new combinations such as:*

> *If it keeps raining like this,*
> *Then she'll never get over it.*

or

> *If he leaves her now,*
> *Then surely one door will open.*

297 *Now choose the most striking or unusual combination to start off, or to use in, a completely new piece of writing.*

Interestingly, we expect writing to be more consequential than life. We like one thing to follow one clearly from another in fiction. Truth is far stranger: real life is often unpredictable and terribly random.

DON'T LOOK!

Using oddly random prompts to start your stories

Before you look at any of the numbered tasks, write down, as quickly as you can, without thinking, answers to these seven prompts:

- an item of kitchen equipment
- a river
- a fruit
- a type of celestial body (sun, moon, star, comet etc)
- a month
- a flavour
- a child's game

These exercises are all about the flexibility of English. You're going to take these words and be adaptable and creative about how you deploy them to tell three different stories.

298 *Use your seven expressions to tell a story about something memorable that has happened to you in the last week.*

299 *Use your seven expressions to tell a story about a moon landing.*

DON'T LOOK!

---

300 *Use your seven expressions to tell a story about a conference, congress or meeting.*

It's not fair to ask you to do something I wouldn't do myself. Here's what happened when I turned my sister into an astronaut. Can you spot my seven words?

It was the first of January when the woman dubbed by the Press and Journal as 'Aberdeen's Astronette' touched down. Fiona Cooper spoke into her communicator. 'Mission Control do you read me?'

'Tangerine Dream this is Mission Control. Copy that.'

Spacewoman Cooper got out her flag. 'Mission Control I am on the Sea of Tranquillity. We have touchdown. Repeat, we have touchdown. The Pear has sprouted!'

Four million ecstatic Scotsmen and women watched as their heroine plunged her flag, marked with its comet logo, into the spacedust. 'In the name of the people of Scotland, I rename this moonscape The Dee of Tranquillity.'

Spacewoman Cooper skipped off across the lunar surface, ready to gather samples in her hand-carved wooden ladle.

PAIN

Making emotional and physical pain worthwhile by writing about it

On Wednesday night at the cinema it felt like a nagging back ache. By Friday morning I was curled up on the bed screaming. I kept retching but I couldn't be sick: every heave was accompanied by a lasso of pain that pulled it back down. My appendix had burst, and by the time surgeons took it out I had developed peritonitis and gangrene. Two weeks later, just when I thought all the agony was over, my lung collapsed. Every breath felt as if someone was stabbing me between the shoulderblades.

I learned from all of this that books had been lying to me. You know that bit in thrillers when the hero has been beaten up by the villains, and the pain makes him black out? As far as I can tell, no matter how hard you wish you could be unconscious, there's no amount of pure pain that will do that to you. But, it does give you plenty of material to write about later.

301 *When you were a child, did you ever hit someone? Tell the story.*

302 *Since you became an adult, have you ever hit someone? Tell the story.*

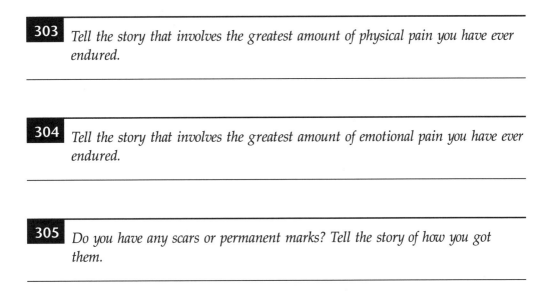

303 *Tell the story that involves the greatest amount of physical pain you have ever endured.*

304 *Tell the story that involves the greatest amount of emotional pain you have ever endured.*

305 *Do you have any scars or permanent marks? Tell the story of how you got them.*

You can give your pain to the fictional characters you write about. As well as writing vividly about what they feel, and what happens to them, think about how you want them to react. It's the way your characters deal with these agonies and challenges that will show your readers what they are like.

MOTIVATIONS

Driving your characters to act

When I'm not writing, I teach high school English. In fact, it would be more accurate to say that when I'm not teaching, I write, as there's only half a day each week when I'm not in school.

Because I love to write, I go to huge lengths to make sure it can happen. I gave up part of my salaried work to create more time. I sometimes write very early in the morning while my husband is still sleeping. I write on the rare weekday evenings when I don't have piles of essays to mark. I am motivated to write and this changes my behaviour. Other priorities fall into place behind this one.

Fictional characters are all motivated by something. If your characters seem flat and lifeless, perhaps you've forgotten to work out what drives them.

306 *Write about a character who is motivated by the need to get revenge.*

307 *Write about a character who is motivated by an unusual fear.*

MOTIVATIONS

308 *Write about a character who is motivated by curiosity.*

309 *Write about a character who is motivated by the need to prove that others are wrong about him or her.*

You probably tackled these tasks as if the characters' motivations were very immediate: that they wanted revenge, or were curious, or felt fear, right now. As the saying goes, though, revenge is a dish best served cold. Would your writing turn out differently if these motivations were actually long term ones? What would revenge be like if the character felt they could wait years for it? How would someone's life turn out if they patiently spent years proving other people's opinions wrong?

A Nasty Surprise

Starting stories with unexpected and unpleasant events

Starting a story with a surprise is a great way to intrigue your readers and draw them in. Earlier in this book, you got a chance to tell stories that began with an unexpected but nice event.

No more Ms (or Mr) Nice Writer. These openings will help you to start stories by unleashing some rather nasty surprises upon your characters.

---

310 *When I arrived at work that morning, armed guards were patrolling the corridors. A voice on the tannoy said, 'Report direct to the canteen. Anyone talking will be shot. Do not attempt to disobey.'*

---

311 *I stuck my hand in the cookie jar. Something furry moved inside. Sharp tiny teeth nipped my finger.*

---

312 *As I popped open the cigarette packet a voice from inside squeaked, 'Don't do it! You'll regret it later!'*

313 *When I got home that night the house door was hanging from its hinges. Yellow police tape slung across it said, 'CRIME SCENE! DO NOT CROSS!' Where were my family?*

One of the classic descriptions of a short story is that it should put its characters through challenges and problems. How did your characters cope with the tests you set them? Did they triumph in the end? Sometimes the hardest, but bravest, thing for a writer to do is to make the reader really like a character, and then make that same reader watch helplessly as the character fails.

SECRETS

Exploring what happens when one character finds out another's secret

We all have secrets. Some of them are entirely innocuous. My husband managed to organise a trip away for my birthday by phoning the B&B, explaining what he was planning, and asking them not to take a deposit because I'd see it on the credit card bill. I organised a party for him by setting up a dedicated Hotmail address and planning the whole thing using emails he knew nothing about. It did strike me though, just for a minute, that that might be how other people manage to get away with having affairs.

All these tasks involve one character finding out another's secrets. You'll need to decide why they come to do this in the first place. Are they already suspicious? Or, is there a completely innocent reason why they are reading someone else's communications?

---

314 *A character reads someone else's diary. What do they discover and what do they do?*

---

315 *A character opens a piece of post addressed to someone else. What do they discover and what do they do?*

---

316 *A character answers their partner's mobile phone. What do they discover and what do they do?*

317 *A character reads the emails in someone else's inbox. What do they discover and what do they do?*

Stories like these offer you the potential to create all sorts of twists. A very suspicious character might jump to the worst possible conclusion about what they read, when it actually has a far more innocent meaning. What happens when one character confronts, or tries to check up on, the other? If character A accuses character B (perhaps wrongly) of some sort of misdemeanor, how does that affect their relationship?

SUMMING UP

Summarising your life in tiny, pithy pieces of writing

Each weekday evening, on his Radio 2 drive time show, Simon Mayo asks his listeners to text in and to sum up their day in three words. Today so far for me is: *Written eight pages.* Yesterday would be: *Term finally ended.* Sunday should, if all goes well, be: *Budapest is beautiful!*

These tasks will get you summing up.

---

318 *Every day for a week, sum up your day in a three-word phrase, as explained above.*

---

319 *Sum up each of the last five years of your life in a three-word phrase.*

---

320 *Sum up each decade of your life so far in a three-word phrase.*

---

321 *Every day for a week, sum up your day by using four nouns.*

322 *Every day for a week, sum up your day by using four adjectives.*

323 *Every day for a week, sum up your day by using four verbs.*

Although this has been a personal writing task, you can use three-word summarising to help you plan your fiction writing. If you're facing up to a scene you want to write, try to think of it first in this kind of shorthand. This will help you to know what's most important about it, and will keep your writing in focus.

RESHAPING

Rewriting other writers' work and making it your own

The band Dire Straits reshaped *Romeo and Juliet* and made it into a pop song, told from the point of view of a still alive, but very jaded, Romeo. Marvel Comics took the Norse god Thor and turned him into a superhero, and later into a movie character in a film directed (slightly surprisingly) by Kenneth Branagh.

These tasks aren't really about adapting something – keeping it broadly the same in a new format. Instead, try for a genuine reshaping. Try to emphasise a facet of the story that is not the one we most immediately think of. You could focus on a different character, or highlight an incident that is relatively unimportant in the original. The original should be your inspiration, but not your raw material.

324 *Rewrite a traditional myth, legend or fairy tale as a tabloid news story.*

325 *Rewrite a traditional fairy tale as a case study, scientific report or doctor's case history.*

326 *Find a cartoon strip of at least three or four frames. Rework it as a story.*

327 *Pick the opening or closing sentence of a novel you love. Use it to start or finish your own different piece of writing.*

Now that you've practised reshaping existing writing, give yourself one more challenge. Go back to a piece of your own writing – maybe one that you always felt didn't quite work – and reshape it. You could change the genre, emphasise a different character, begin or end in a different place or focus on a different event.

IMPOSSIBLE

Questioning the subjects you can't or shouldn't write about

Some topics might seem impossible to write about. How would you handle paedophilia, or suicide? And yet, for every subject in the world, no matter how delicate, someone has found a way to tackle it.

Alan Sillitoe's sad and moving short story *Uncle Ernest* makes the reader sympathise with a lonely old man who is wrongly accused of having unsuitable intentions towards two little girls he meets in a café.

One website lists 72 poems by famous and reputable poets about suicide, and Dorothy Parker somehow even makes the subject seem bleakly funny in her poem *Resume*. She lists the unsatisfactory nature of possible methods before concluding: *'You might as well live.'*

We might even say that while there are difficult, or delicate, subjects, there are no taboo ones. It's just down to how well you write about them.

328 *What do you think are the delicate, or perhaps impossible subjects? Make a list.*

329 *Pick the hardest-looking topic off your list. Spend some time researching it. Which groups exist to campaign or inform on this issue? How has it cropped up in the news lately? How has it affected your own family or friends? How has it been tackled in literature? What else can you find out?*

330 *Now plan how you could deal with the subject. As a poem? A newspaper opinion column or essay? A story, whose characters experience the issue for themselves?*

331 *Now at last, write your piece.*

Did you prove to yourself that no subject is impossible?

JUST 6 WORDS

Telling the shortest of stories

Ernest Hemingway once said his best work was a story he wrote in just six words:

For sale: baby shoes, never worn.

It works because it tells a whole story by making you work out the sad and complex tale behind the few simple words.

The Arvon Foundation, which runs fantastic residential writing courses in quiet country houses, ran a six word story competition. These are some of the entries I sent:

Dead body. Merry widow. Case closed.

Baby. Bath water. Gin. No baby.

Happy, ever. After? End of story.

"Hello darling, it's me."
"Sorry, who?"

Loved a surrealist. He melted away.

The winning story in the Arvon competition was:

We buried the whale at night.

This fascinated me so much that I adapted it as the final line of a story I went on to write about what had happened to that whale.

JUST 6 WORDS

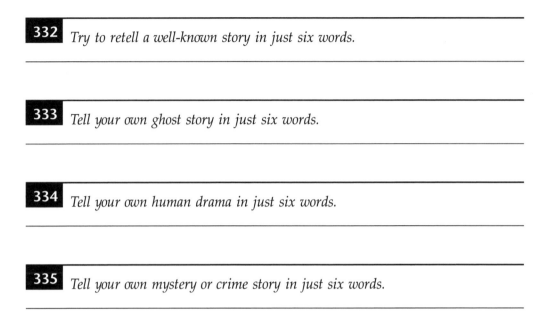

332 *Try to retell a well-known story in just six words.*

333 *Tell your own ghost story in just six words.*

334 *Tell your own human drama in just six words.*

335 *Tell your own mystery or crime story in just six words.*

How well did your stories work in implying the longer, more complex tales that lurked behind them?

LOVELY LISTS 3

Using more lists to make you see things differently

In her poem *'You're'*, Sylvia Plath creates a list of descriptions of her unborn first child. Some are similes: the baby is *'Gilled like a fish'*. Some are metaphors: she calls her child, *'high-riser, my little loaf'*. Some lines describe how the baby feels as it moves inside her, such as, *'all ripples'*.

Here are four more chances to make lists. Spend a few minutes on each one. Let your imagination, and your love of language, lead you. Try to write something nobody else would think of. Be delightfully oblique. What should you never regret? A kiss. What comes out of the sky? The frozen contents of aeroplane toilets. What tends to fall apart? Cheap shoes just when you need to strut your stuff.

336 *Make a list of things you should never regret.*

337 *Make a list of things that come out of the sky.*

LOVELY LISTS 3

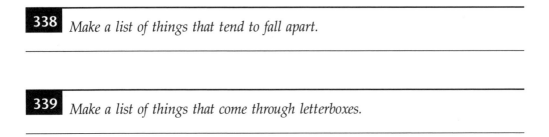

338 *Make a list of things that tend to fall apart.*

339 *Make a list of things that come through letterboxes.*

If you haven't had a chance to, do look up the Plath poem, and Christopher Smart's, *'For I Will Consider My Cat Jeoffry'*, which was mentioned in the earlier listing task.

Once you've read the Plath, which really is stuffed full of similes and metaphors, go back to your own lists. Can any of the items be rephrased to use these sorts of imagery? What would you like to do with these lists now?

Learn From Success

Finding guidance for your writing in the work of others

You sometimes hear writers say that don't read much because they want their own work to be original. But, if your work is utterly unlike anything that has ever been published, it's unlikely anybody will ever want to publish it! Anyway, a writer who doesn't read makes about as much sense as a chef who never eats, or a musician who goes around with cotton wool stuffed in his ears.

340 *Read the book review section of a paper like* The Guardian. *Find an intriguing review of a first novel by a new writer. Buy the book and read it. What made a publisher take a chance on this unknown?*

341 *Find a bestselling book from the year you were born and read it. What do you think made it so popular all those years ago? Do you think this book would still be a success now? What can you take from it to guide your own writing?*

342 *Read the book at the top of this week's paperback fiction bestseller lists. What can you learn from it? What is it about this story, and about how it is told, that has made so many people want to read it?*

343 *The Man Booker prize is given to the novel of the year. The Forward Prize honours poets. The Orange Prize is for women's writing and the Costa picks a book of the year that can even be non-fiction. Read a recent prize winner. What do you think made the judges like this book so much?*

What you read will guide you in how to write. It will help you to know what works, and what doesn't.

WHAT IF? 3

Using more hypothetical situations to kick off stories

Some of the stories I have most enjoyed writing began with a *'What if?'* What if a retired couple embrace self-sufficiency? What if a pop star fakes his own death? What if an ambitious young man decides to gentrify a crumbling old house?

These *'What if?'* questions will start your stories off. If you have a friend to work with, it can be a good idea to brainstorm all the possible things that might follow from this first event. Once you've got a good long list, pick the ideas you'd like to use in your writing.

344 *What if someone decides to follow his/her horoscope for the day?*

345 *What if an angel crash-lands on earth?*

---

346 *What if someone knocks on the door, late on a cold, dark, snowy night? Is the story different if the person in the house is alone?*

---

347 *What if a microscopic world of tiny creatures lives in your doormat, hairbrush or plughole?*

When I explored my questions, I found out that a few pigs at the bottom of the garden might well have carnivorous urges. It's not easy to live a quiet life if you're used to singing to, and being adored by, crowds of thousands. Houses don't enjoy being renovated: they fight back in sinister ways.

What did you find out as you answered your questions?

PROVOCATIONS

Following on from spiky opening dialogue

I have a friend I am dearly attached to. She's hard-working and would do anything for anyone. She's a brilliant cook and hostess. I'm sure she's kind to animals. Yet, if I was being totally honest, I'd have to say that her default setting is 'spiky'. She's so easily provoked, and is always just a little bit prickly.

We can all be that way sometimes. These openings will get you to start with a line of spiky, combative, provocative dialogue. Put the words in the mouth of a character. It's up to you whether you use them to start off a story or a piece of scriptwriting. The advantage either way is that you will get right into the situation with no padding.

---

348 *Use these opening words and follow on from them: 'A glass of tap water would have been fine'*

---

349 *Follow on from this opening: 'You know what? I honestly don't care'*

---

350 *Follow on from this opening: 'I know they've all been lying to you about me'*

---

351 *Follow on from this opening: 'Why didn't you call me?'*

If you look at writing advice sites on the internet (which can be a very confusing thing to do) you'll find some that tell you very firmly never to start a story with dialogue. Obviously, I don't believe this, or I wouldn't have asked you to try these exercises.

But, if you start with dialogue, you do need to be careful where you go next. The challenge is to make clear for the reader, as soon as possible, where and when the story is happening and who is involved in it.

To check if you've been able to do this, show your writing to a trusted friend and ask them to tell you honestly if anything is confusing or under explained.

GIVING LIFE 2

Imagining the lives of other people's characters

Earlier in the book you took real people you hardly knew, and turned them into believable fictions. You can play around with fictional characters too. Jean Rhys gave life to a minor character in her novel *Wide Sargasso Sea*. She took the first Mrs Rochester from *Jane Eyre*, the *'mad woman in the attic'* and wrote her story, giving the reader new sympathy for someone who was feared and misunderstood.

352 *Take two characters you liked from different books. Write a piece in which they meet. What happens? Or, write about a dinner party where all the guests are characters from different works of fiction.*

353 *Choose a key character from a book, or film. Write about their life and adventures ten years after the end of the existing story.*

354 *Pick a minor character from a work of fiction: a servant from a Victorian novel; the not so pretty friend of the romantic heroine and so on. Then, either tell the existing story from this character's point of view, or create a whole new story which is actually about them.*

355 *Find a famous fictional villain. Let this person persuade us that they are innocent, or just misunderstood, or that they are actually the victim.*

If you'd like to see how one author breathes fantastic new life into a host of pre-existing characters, read Jasper Fforde's novels about the literary detective Thursday Next. There's a great moment in *The Well of Lost Plots* where she has to conduct an anger management session for the cast of *Wuthering Heights*.

FLASHBACKS 4

Working out what brought more characters to a certain point

You might think that the flashback is a tricksy, new-fangled technique, perhaps invented by film makers or post-modern novelists. In fact, Emily Brontë's *Wuthering Heights*, published in 1847, is built round a flashback. Though the first three and last three chapters are narrated by Mr Lockwood, the bulk of the story is a flashback told to him by his housekeeper Nelly Dean. She explains the long, sad story of Heathcliff and Catherine to him after he spends a frightening night at Wuthering Heights.

Here are four final dramatic situations that are just begging to be explained in a flashback.

356 *I took a sip of wine. It was boiling hot and burned my throat. I gulped a spoonful of ice cream then spat it out immediately when I realised that it was hotter than a Vindaloo.*

357 *'I'll never trust anyone again,' I thought, as I dropped his/her photo in the bin.*

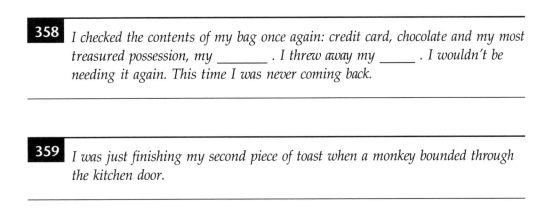

358 *I checked the contents of my bag once again: credit card, chocolate and my most treasured possession, my _____ . I threw away my _____ . I wouldn't be needing it again. This time I was never coming back.*

359 *I was just finishing my second piece of toast when a monkey bounded through the kitchen door.*

You may have found that the flashbacks did not all need to be the same length. Some of the extracts probably felt as if they came from near the start of their stories, and just needed a small amount of explanation. Others will need quite a lot of backstory to make them make sense.

One last challenge, even if you can't, or don't want to, write the whole of these stories: which two sentences could you write after each of the originals I gave you to get the rest of the story moving forwards?

Remember Me

Considering how you, and your writing, will be remembered

At the school where I work, we had, for a few months, a supply teacher who became a bit of a legend. He used to turn all the classroom lights off and sit on the front desk telling the pupils stories about his criminal past. Nobody ever forgot him, but nobody learned anything. Another colleague had a classroom like an all-consuming black hole. Six months after he left, we found all our laptop computers in one of his cupboards.

---

360 *It's six months since you left your workplace. How would your colleagues describe you if asked by a new member of staff who'd never met you?*

---

361 *What words will be written on your gravestone?*

---

362 *Read some newspaper obituaries. Try to choose ones about people you'd never heard of, so the obituary tells you everything you know about them. Once you have a feel for how this kind of writing works, write one about yourself.*

363 *What would someone who was at primary school with you remember? What about someone who was in your class at secondary school?*

This kind of writing can be useful just as it is, as a personal task. It can also be a good exercise to work through for fictional characters you are creating.

One more thing to think about: what would your readers remember, and say, about your writing?

KEEP WRITING!

Finding more and more ways to write, and to share your writing

You may not be able to call yourself an author until you've been published, but you're always a writer as long as you're writing. Here are some suggestions to keep you going.

---

364 *Doing these things will help you to develop your writing:*

- *Carry a notebook everywhere to note down ideas and observations.*
- *Write every day, or at least every week.*
- *Join a class: your local university and education department probably run evening classes.*
- *Go on a writing holiday: the week-long courses run by the Arvon Foundation changed my life.*
- *Subscribe to a writer's magazine:* The New Writer *publishes lots of its readers' work, and* Mslexia *is brilliant for woman writers.*

---

365 *Doing these things will help you to share your work:*

- *Share your work with friends who care about you, asking them to make at least one constructive suggestion for how you could change it.*
- *Share your work with other writers: listen to their suggestions about your work, and make suggestions in turn about theirs.*
- *Join a writers' group: your local library may be able to put you in contact with one.*
- *Submit your work to magazines, and enter competitions.*

At the start of this book I said that sometimes we don't know what to write, and sometimes we don't know how to write well. I hope that all these exercises and prompts have helped you get round these two problems. All you have to do now is, keep writing!